"An important book. Mark Labberton offers a scalding reminder that worship is not about our well-being but the world's. I can't imagine any worship leader, or any worshiper, seeing worship in the same way after reading this book."

TIM STAFFORD, SENIOR WRITER, *CHRISTIANITY TODAY*, AND AUTHOR OF *SURPRISED BY JESUS*

"This prophetic, passionate and thoroughly biblical exploration of the connection between genuine worship and God's call to justice breaks new ground in a much-needed wake-up call for the American church. With insightful critique and practical examples, it encourages Christians to move beyond the often stale and sterile debates of the worship wars to the rediscovery of world- and life-changing God-centered worship. I highly recommend it."

THE REV. DR. ROBERTA HESTENES, TEACHING PASTOR, COMMUNITY PRESBYTERIAN CHURCH, DANVILLE, CALIFORNIA, AND FORMER MINISTER-AT-LARGE FOR WORLD VISION

"In *The Dangerous Act of Worship: Living God's Call to Justice*, Mark Labberton gives a compelling argument on the connection between worshiper and justice. Mark packs in lots of living examples of worshipers who are doing justice in the world. The church in North America desperately needs to catch Mark's (and God's) passion for giving away the mercy that we have so richly received to the marginalized people of our world, both near and far."

ANDY PARK, WORSHIP LEADER, SONGWRITER AND AUTHOR OF *TO KNOW YOU MORE*

"Mark Labberton writes with the voice of a prophet and the heart of a pastor. His call for justice forges links between corporate worship on Sunday and personal worship in all of life. His call to genuine gospel rest in the context of a book arising from a holy restlessness sets this book apart from many books on justice. The result is a book that calls us to obedient service not on the basis of fear or guilt, but rather deep gratitude for God's abundant grace."

JOHN D. WITVLIET, DIRECTOR, CALVIN INSTITUTE OF CHRISTIAN WORSHIP

"Why *do* churches fight over the small stuff and miss the big issues of justice and mercy? In this book not only does Mark Labberton help us to ask that question, but also he poses it more thoroughly and challenges us to find the resources to do something about the problem. This book is essential for awakening churches from their 'yet more excellent sleep' to their role in living the gospel that they proclaim and thereby in changing the state of the world."

MARVA DAWN, AUTHOR OF *REACHING OUT WITHOUT DUMBING DOWN* AND *UNFETTERED HOPE: A CALL TO FAITHFUL LIVING IN AN AFFLUENT CULTURE*, AND TEACHING FELLOW IN SPIRITUAL THEOLOGY, REGENT COLLEGE, VANCOUVER

"We need this book! Mark Labberton offers profound insights and guidance to all of us who care deeply—or at least who ought to care deeply—about promoting justice in a suffering world. He is right: integrating worship and justice is a dangerous thing. But given the character of the God whom we worship it is also the only safe course of action."

RICHARD J. MOUW, PRESIDENT AND PROFESSOR OF CHRISTIAN PHILOSOPHY, FULLER THEOLOGICAL SEMINARY

"Dangerous indeed! Not only is true worship dangerous, as Mark Labberton suggests, but this book is dangerous. It shakes us from our lethargy. It calls us to a radical reconsideration of our life of discipleship. It pushes us across our global and theological boundaries. This is one of the most challenging books I have read in years."

STEPHEN A. HAYNER, PROFESSOR OF EVANGELISM AND CHURCH GROWTH, COLUMBIA THEOLOGICAL SEMINARY

"This is not just another book on worship. Or justice. It's an urgent call to wake up to the discovery that everything is lost unless we pull worship and justice together."

M. CRAIG BARNES, PROFESSOR OF PASTORAL MINISTRY, PITTSBURGH SEMINARY, AND AUTHOR OF YEARNING AND WHEN GOD INTERRUPTS

"For those of us who are unsettled by popular worship, narrowly defined, Mark Labberton calls us to wake up and see that worship can never be understood narrowly. It must be part of the fabric of our faith, woven into larger issues like justice and the poor. Though he does not give into the temptation of entering into the debate over secondary issues of style and personal preference, Mark's words provide the biblical background that will place them finally into proper focus."

MICHAEL CARD, MUSICIAN, SONGWRITER AND AUTHOR OF SCRIBBLING IN THE SAND

"Few topics arouse such emotion and passion in the church as the place of justice and worship. Mark dares to bring them together, and does it masterfully. Neither a critic of the church—standing aloof and pointing a finger—nor a comforter—standing alongside and holding in an embrace—rather Mark is a prophetic pastor. He compassionately discloses the will and the way of God and invites us to walk together in the way of God's kingdom. This book is discomforting. And well it should be. Mark restores our vision of God's ancient call to the church to do justice, love mercy and walk humbly. The book opens the windows so God's Spirit can blow fresh joy and power into our lives. Rather than worship being a weekly separation from the world, Mark leads us into worship as a daily, transforming engagement with it."

TIM DEARBORN, ASSOCIATE DIRECTOR, CHRISTIAN COMMITMENTS/FAITH AND DEVELOPMENT, WORLD VISION INTERNATIONAL

MARK LABBERTON

Foreword by JOHN ORTBERG

THE DANGEROUS ACT OF
WORSHIP

Living God's Call to Justice

IVP Books

An imprint of InterVarsity Press
Downers Grove, Illinois

InterVarsity Press
P.O. Box 1400, Downers Grove, IL 60515-1426
World Wide Web: www.ivpress.com
E-mail: email@ivpress.com

InterVarsity Press® is the book-publishing division of InterVarsity Christian Fellowship/USA®, a movement of students and faculty active on campus at hundreds of universities, colleges and schools of nursing in the United States of America, and a member movement of the International Fellowship of Evangelical Students. For information about local and regional activities, write Public Relations Dept., InterVarsity Christian Fellowship/USA, 6400 Schroeder Rd., P.O. Box 7895, Madison, WI 53707-7895, or visit the IVCF website at <www.intervarsity.org>.

Scripture quotations, unless otherwise noted, are from the New Revised Standard Version of the Bible, copyright 1989 by the Division of Christian Education of the National Council of the Churches of Christ in the USA. Used by permission. All rights reserved.

Cover Design:Cindy Kiple
Image: © Oleksiy Tsuper/iStockphoto

ISBN 978-0-8308-3414-3

Printed in the United States of America ∞

 InterVarsity Press is committed to protecting the environment and to the responsible use of natural resources. As a member of the Green Press Initiative we use recycled paper whenever possible. To learn more about the Green Press Initiative, visit <www.greenpressinitiative.org>.

Library of Congress Cataloging-in-Publication Data

Labberton, Mark, 1953-
   The dangerous act of worship: living God's call to justice / Mark
Labberton.
      p. cm.
   Includes bibliographical references.
   ISBN-13: 978-0-8308-3316-0 (cloth: alk. paper)
   ISBN-10: 0-8308-3316-1 (cloth: alk. paper)
   1. Worship. 2. Christian life. 3. Social justice—Religious
aspects—Christianity. I. Title.
   BV10.3.L33 2007
   264—dc22

                                                                2006038974

| P | 19 | 18 | 17 | 16 | 15 | 14 | 13 | 12 | 11 | 10 | 9 | 8 | 7 | 6 | 5 | 4 | 3 | 2 | 1 |
| Y | 28 | 27 | 26 | 25 | 24 | 23 | 22 | 21 | 20 | 19 | 18 | 17 | 16 | 15 | 14 | 13 | 12 |

Contents

Foreword by John Ortberg 7

Acknowledgments 11

1   What's at Stake in Worship? 13

2   The Real Battle over Worship 21

3   False Dangers 41

4   Real Dangers 61

5   Waking Up to Where We Live 78

6   Doing Justice Starts with Rest 95

7   When Worship Talks to Power 109

8   Dwelling in Exodus or in Exile? 132

9   An Imagination for Justice 148

10   Living Awake 168

Epilogue 188

Study Guide 190

Notes 199

Foreword

NOBODY EVER WENT UP TO JESUS AFTER HIS blistering warning about religious hypocrisy and shook his hand and said, "Thanks, rabbi. That was a nice talk."

Nobody went up to Moses after the thunder, lightning and loud trumpet blast at the foot of Mount Sinai and said, "How come we're using trumpets now? What happened to Miriam and that tambourine song we used to sing crossing the Red Sea? I liked that song—it was peppy. This thunder and trumpet stuff is too heavy."

Nobody came up to Solomon after the ark had been brought to the temple when it was surrounded by the cloud of glory and said, "You know, this cloud of glory is keeping the priests from getting their job done. Nobody told us that if we contributed to the capital campaign for the new temple that there would be fog involved."

At least, no one made the comments as far as we know. On the other hand, human nature being what it is, it would be nice to know more details of harebrained responses to worship in the ancient world. There must have been some. Somebody proposed the golden calf. David's wife felt he went a little Pentecostal in his liturgical dancing.

But the general sense that occurs in the writings of Scripture is that when God shows up, people get blown away. They fall to the ground, they hide their face, they get radiant like light bulbs, they beg for mercy: "Away from me, Lord, I am a sinful man." They "stayed at a distance and said to Moses, 'Speak to us yourself and we will listen, but do not have God speak to us or we will die.'"

It is this sense of worship as the often fearful, overwhelmed, convicted, transported, sometimes euphoric response to the disruptive Presence that Mark Labberton calls us to. He wants us to think about worship not as a service we attend occasionally but as the life-altering recognition that Someone has shown up and changed the rules that our society tells us govern human existence. Worship, he says, is to be the new way of seeing and feeling that redraws boundaries, rewires connections and redistricts how we govern ourselves. It subverts the way we decide who counts and who doesn't.

In our day the phrase "worship wars" has become a familiar one to certain churches, although there is surely something oxymoronic about it. There are many views on the battles and questions that go on over aspects of style in worship, particularly around music. I don't think those are unimportant questions. Yale professor Nicholas Wolterstorff once said that each people group, each generation, needs to be able to express its sense of worship in its own voice, in a way that can resonate deep in the soul. And as our culture (or conglomeration of subcultures) keeps changing, these are not issues that the church can pretend will go away sometime soon.

But Mark wants us to think about something deeper. For even if there was an era where everybody in Christendom was using the same Gregorian chants, it does not mean that the ultimate worship challenge was solved. Mark wants us to understand that the profound questions that worship raises are, in a sense, masked by discussions of style or delivery systems.

So this book is a bell from the warning tower. It is a summons to consider how we—not just the people who attend our churches but also those of us who lead them—can listen to what the Spirit is saying in our day. It is an alarm clock telling us the sun has already risen: "Wake up, O sleeper, rise from the dead, and Christ will shine on you." And worship is what happens when people wake up. But worship must never be a series of isolated liturgical communal acts. It is to be embedded in a wakeful day.

The prophet Micah said a long time ago that the divine requirements for human life are not rocket science: Do justice, love mercy and walk humbly before your God. Worship is the humble walk. It is the knee-buckling, jaw-dropping acknowledgment of the gap between the creature and the Creator, the finite and the Infinite, the sinful and the Holy. It is the heart-rending, spirit-mending gratitude and joy of those who have tasted the wonder that words like *redemption* can only hint at.

But apart from doing justice and loving mercy, worship means no more than a child's "thank you" means if it is accompanied with a selfish unwillingness to share what she claims to be thankful for. To paraphrase Gloria Steinem, a passion for worship goes with an indifference to justice like a fish goes with a bicycle.

So, enough with the prelims. Mark writes this not only with thoughtful passion but also with the wisdom of a practitioner. He actually has to help people engage in worship all the time. He is a wise guide. Read him and change.

John Ortberg
Teaching Pastor, Menlo Park Presbyterian Church

Acknowledgments

LIKE THE REST OF MY LIFE, THIS BOOK CAN ONLY BE EXPLAINED by a combination of the grace of God and the love of family and friends. I want, first and foremost, to thank the remarkable woman who is my wife, Janet, for her invaluable love and support, as well as our two sons, Peter and Sam, for their patience and encouragement. My parents, Wells and Jean, were better witnesses to the heart of God than I ever knew growing up, and I am deeply grateful to them, as well as for my brother, Kurt, who continues to be one of my greatest mentors and friends.

Steve Hayner and Tim Dearborn have also been formative and healing teachers and friends; our triumvirate is far beyond a common grace, and we know it. Gary Haugen holds a unique place in my heart for his tenderness, courage and hope.

John Stott's global heart and vision reflect the gospel to me in liberating and profound ways. For such a significant Christian leader to be more impressive the more one knows of him is in itself evidence of God's grace. I am enormously grateful for his example, his teaching and his friendship, which have faithfully embodied the themes in this book.

Honest feedback in the writing process has been invaluable. In addition to feedback from Janet, Kurt, Steve, Tim and Gary, I am also grateful to Tom Boyce, Joyce French, Mary Graves, Thomas Kelley, Rick Mayes, Richard Mouw, Zac Niringiye, Tim Stafford and Joel Wickre. Michael Barram's exceptional generosity and help have meant a lot. Of course, all weaknesses and inadequacies of the final product are mine.

Generous friendship has also been so influential in shaping me and in enlarging my heart for the world. I am especially indebted to Marc Nikkel, who in his life and death pointed me, and many Dinka in Sudan, ever more deeply to God and to the world. I am also indebted to others: Dave Anderson, Craig Barnes, Marta Bennett, Assayehen Berhe, Paul Bryant, Andy Crouch, Phillippe Daniel, Brian Morris, Gladys and Gershon Mwiti, Ng Kam Weng, Tim Teusink, Vinoth Ramachandra, and Amy Sherman.

Since this is my first book, the editors at IVP have had to cope with the learning curve I've gone through. I am grateful for the hard work of the InterVarsity Press staff and, especially, to Al Hsu.

The First Presbyterian Church of Berkeley has been my primary church home for the past twenty-five years, and Janet and I are the fourth generation (in her family) to meet and marry there. If love "bears all things, believes all things, hopes all things, endures all thing," this community has certainly demonstrated such love toward me over these years. The encouragement and support of the congregation, of the elders and of the staff have meant more than I can say. Barbara Allen, Michael Brooks, Tim Buscheck, Bob Russell, Aileen Schier and Ruth Traylor have been such important encouragers. I want particularly to thank my treasured pastoral colleagues: Mary Ellen Azada, Erik Hanson, Josh McPaul, Tim Shaw and Debbie Whaley. Finally, I want to thank Julie Sept, whose highly capable and devoted staff partnership makes writing possible, and Patti Nicolson who, along with Jesus Christ, "holds all things together"!

1   What's at Stake in Worship?

EVERYTHING. THAT'S WHAT'S AT STAKE IN WORSHIP. The urgent, indeed troubling, message of Scripture is that everything that matters is at stake in worship.

Worship names what matters most: the way human beings are created to reflect God's glory by embodying God's character in lives that seek righteousness and do justice. Such comprehensive worship redefines all we call ordinary. Worship turns out to be the dangerous act of waking up to God and to the purposes of God in the world, and then living lives that actually show it.

Worship, then, refers to something very big and very small, and much in between. It can point to the meaning and work of the whole created order. Worship can also be in the cry of a mother or in the joy of a new disciple. Worship can name a Sunday gathering of God's people, but it also includes how we treat those around us, how we spend our money, and how we care for the lost and the oppressed. Worship can encompass every dimension of our lives.

True worship includes the glory and honor due God—Father, Son, and Spirit. It also includes the enactment of God's love and justice, mercy and kindness in the world. This is the encounter and the transformation that is worth the pearl of great price, both for our sake and for our neighbor's. On the one hand, Scripture indicates that worship is meant to be the tangible embodiment of God's hope in the world. Conversely, the Bible also teaches that the realities of oppression, poverty and injustice can be both a call to worship and an indictment of our failure to do so.

Clearly we are not primarily speaking about *worship* here in the limited but important sense of the *service of worship,* though we will certainly reflect on that. Nor do we mean a still smaller piece of that service, the period of extended singing that is distinct from prayer and preaching that some call worship. This is not a book about postmodern worship versus modern worship. We are not concerned here with the pros and cons of praise choruses versus hymns, nor with liturgical debates over the value of candles, video clips, worship cafés or special lighting. These issues are not the focus of this book, although they may be as far as some have gone in considering the subject of worship. And that is part of what this book will try to change.

When worship is our response to the One who alone is worthy of it—Jesus Christ—then our lives are on their way to being turned inside out. Every dimension of self-centered living becomes endangered as we come to share God's self-giving heart. Worship exposes our cultural and even spiritual complacency toward a world of suffering and injustice. In Jesus Christ, we are called into a new kind of living. Through the grace of worship, God applies the necessary antidote to what we assume is merely human—our selfishness. Worship sets us free from ourselves to be free for God and God's purposes in the world. The dangerous act of worshiping God in Jesus Christ necessarily draws us into the heart of God and sends us out to embody it, especially toward the poor, the forgotten and the oppressed. All of this is what matters most and is most at stake in worship.

So what's the problem? The church is asleep. Not dead. Not necessarily having trouble breathing. But asleep. This puts everything that matters at stake: God's purposes in the church and in the world.

Whether I think of myself, or congregations I have served as a pastor, or other churches across the country and around the world, it seems that many of us are asleep to God's heart for a world filled with injustice. It's no surprise that we also seem to be asleep to God's desire that out of worship should come a church that seeks and embodies the justice that's needed in the world. We are asleep to God's heart for the poor and oppressed, absorbed with our own inner life, wrestling with our own dreams and traumas that, for all their vividness, are unknown, unseen and largely unreal to the world around us.

I offer these observations first as a personal confession. *Slumber* would not be far off the mark in describing my own vision and heart toward the world at times. Busy with life, preoccupied with ministry, absorbed with what is personal, local, immediate—it's easy to feel like there is not enough of me to go around as it is! So the thought of deliberately seeking to engage beyond these aspects of life can easily be neglected. Left to my own devices, I can live quite contentedly inside the bubble of my middle-class American life. Little in my world, apart from the presence and power of the gospel itself, would ever really demand or expect that I look beyond it. In clearer moments, I know this is a kind of sleepwalking. I write as one who is still just awakening yet who is eager for others to join in imitating those who are truly awake.

Beyond my own personal confession, my obversations of other Christians and churches and the absence of any strong evidence to the contrary convinces me that the church is largely asleep—even if it doesn't look like it. For example, I recently stood on the grounds of a remarkable church: vibrant, thoughtful, committed, engaged, creative. It was the first day of an enormous, richly choreographed vacation Bible school program. Amid the swirl of activity, I watched the children in color-coordinated orange T-shirts dance and follow the worship band, whose faces were also projected larger than life on two huge screens up front.

Suddenly I felt that these hundreds of children were being put spiritually asleep—asleep to the God of the still small voice, to the God who suffered for the sake of the world, to the God who said, "Lay down your life, take up your cross, and follow me." Don't get me wrong; I do not doubt for a moment that the VBS leaders intended just the opposite. They were simply trying to find the best means to communicate to the children. But instead, what seemed evident to me was that this church, one that would by most measures be considered *awake,* was running the risk of investing astonishing energy in breeding and nurturing a yet more excellent sleep. Why? Because the primary message of its building, its programs and its ministry announced that it was first and foremost an institution that was wealthy and white. The church's sociology was the primary message. The VBS production featured everything money and time could buy and was so central and primary that the gospel felt small and incidental in comparison. It felt like an instance of Jesus "in distressing disguise," indeed possibly beyond recognition.

Even more unnerving, I had to acknowledge that this could just as easily and just as well be said of the vibrant church that I pastor. My church's subculture is different, but not on a global scale. We have just finished a major building campaign and have enhanced our facilities substantially, with many years of effort and much expense. The privileges of churches like these can shroud the gospel in such middle- and upper-class consumer-oriented style and content that salvation subtly becomes more about providing a warm blanket of cultural safety than about stepping out into the bracing winds of spiritual sacrifice. Such patterns in a church's life can easily, if unintentionally, lead to a focus on consolidating and extending power instead of identifying with the powerless. The former is a lot more like a comfortable bed to sleep in than the latter. No wonder we don't want to wake up, let alone get up and get going in the work of justice.

It is too ambiguous to speak about the church in the United States as one large, encumbered entity. It is not. It encompasses various denominations and congregations, each with its own subcultures, groups and theologies. Examples of vivid wakefulness can be found—Christians and congregations whose lives are daily demonstrations of God's heart for justice. However, it still seems broadly the case that either the church is asleep or it may as well be. When measured against the global realities of life on planet Earth that silently scream for attention, the vast institutional life of American Protestantism seems functionally distant and disengaged. According to Scripture, that's an issue of worship. According to much church culture, there's no connection between worship and justice.

Many denominations are declining in membership, mine—the Presbyterian Church (USA)—most of all. Each denomination has its own battles over various issues of the culture wars, seeking to be faithful to its traditions and convictions while at the same time trying to respond to today's circumstances. These discussions are largely internal, often passionate, frequently wounding and alienating to those inside the church but distant and disconnected to those outside it. Meanwhile, on a local level congregations require tending. Individuals and families have needs and crises. When our own immediate world overwhelms us, we can readily feel disinclined or unable to look beyond it.

When we do look beyond, however, we see vividly that the daily lives of millions of people around the world are about chronic desperation. The world is racked with dramatic, torturous suffering as a consequence of poverty and injustice—from human trafficking to HIV/AIDS, from malnutrition to genocide. One-sixth of the world's population lives in absolute poverty,[1] and nearly a million children each year are sold or forced into the sex-trafficking trade.[2] But this is not just about statistics—it's about real lives. People with names and families are living daily without food or water, in sickness or oppression. Their experience is in their bodies and hearts and minds, not in a global facts chart. They are made with the same dignity and worth as you and me. They have the same capacities and desires. But they are circumstantially without hope. Every day.

All this is going on while mainline and evangelical churches keep debating what they think are the primary worship issues: guitars versus organs, formal versus informal, traditional versus contemporary, contemporary versus emergent; while other denominations are absorbed in debates over issues like gay and lesbian ordination that dominate their landscapes and preoccupy their fading national bureaucracies; and while congregations and individuals alike struggle with their own needs, genuine and personal as they are.

At a time when many are struck by the polarization between liberal and evangelical churches in America, it is more striking to see what the average congregations on both sides hold in common: they are asleep. Some seem asleep to God. Some seem asleep to the world. Some sleep on their right side, others on their left, but either way they are asleep. The way they sleep, the character of their dreams, the forms of their sleepwalking or sleep-talking varies. Varied, too, are the words and voices that cause restlessness, making their sleep less than tranquil: *Inclusivity. Diversity. Faithfulness. Process. Power. Justice. Relevance. Recovery. Healing. Biblical.* The words may stir the sleeping, but without enough urgency to demand awakening.

Too much sleep can lead to enervation and, in time, atrophy. A crisis hits—9/11 or the Asian tsunami or Hurricane Katrina, say—and like waking from a deep sleep or shaken by a nightmare, our churches raise their heads and try to rise to the occasion (if they can figure out what it is!). Before long, the clamor of crisis quiets down, and our desire to return to the safe coziness of familiarity is too hard to resist. Wakefulness demands too much energy or strength that cannot be mustered or sustained.

Some Christians and some congregations seem to have selective wakefulness. After all, we are weary, overwhelmed, insecure, internally longing for hope of our own (never mind the need for hope in the world). We don't see much beyond the edges of our own bed, whether it is culture, economics, race, denomination or class. We know and like our bed. We have made it. We are not inclined to leave it. We are entitled to it after all, since we see it as God's blessing.

Meanwhile, those without a bed—and without a home, food, safety, water, warmth or knowledge of the Savior's love—are not seen or remembered or reached. In light of the stark reality of lost and dying humanity, forced prostitution, bonded slavery, malarial epidemics, HIV/ AIDS and human life stripped of its dignity around the globe, where is the evidence that through worship our lives have actually been redefined and realigned with God's heart for justice in the world?

Many of us want to remain asleep. Pastors have in part fostered this somnambulating life with preaching that avoids problems and prophets, controversy and complexity. When preaching plays to the culture without substantially critiquing and engaging it, it becomes part of the problem. Sermons that only apply to the individual and to the inner life of the disciple without raising biblical questions about our public lives are also a factor. So, too, are worship services that offer little more than comfort food: the baked potatoes of love, the melting butter of grace, with just enough bacon and chives of outreach to ease the conscience. All this becomes a churchly anesthetic.

I grew up at the edge of church life, believing that pastors were people who attended to a world of very small things with obsessive care. Now that I am a pastor and work among many other pastors, I confess that this is often true, although perhaps by habit rather than desire. The projects and preoccupations of each day can keep me more than busy. Like most pastors, I want to be a faithful shepherd. I want to focus on the call right before me. That can easily seem like too much on most days, but it can also be small and myopic. It lends itself to sleepwalking, which is already too attractive to many of those we lead.

Jesus, if anything, was and is awake. That's the shock for those who encounter him in the Gospels. He came to make a world of those who are awake—awake to God, to each other and to the world. Waking up is the dangerous act of worship. It's dangerous because worship is meant to produce lives fully attentive to reality as God sees it, and that's more

than most of us want to deal with. Yes, true worship always questions
the dominant paradigms, even those within the church. It asks whether
we are bowing before reality or falsehood, before God or idols.

One of the most dramatic periods of Israel's history came about because of the nation's failure to live its worship. God's criticism of Israel
was that it professed what it failed to live. It went through the external
signs of worship but failed to live out what the worship was meant to
show. The Old Testament prophet Micah distilled Israel's call at that critical time:

> What does the LORD require of you
> but to do justice, and to love kindness,
>   and to walk humbly with your God? (Micah 6:8)

Though frequently quoted, these words are meant to be lived. To do
so means we must wake up.

God longs for the church to be awake. God's grace understands our
slumber, while shaking us into wakeful action. The extreme cost of our
delirium denies God what is deserved, distorts our humanity and undermines God's mission in the world. In this book we will consider why and
how the disconnection between worship and justice exists as it does,
how a more vigorous and encompassing theology of worship can help
wake us up, and how faithful worship means finding our life in God and
practicing that life in the world, especially for the sake of the poor, the
oppressed and the forgotten.

2 The Real Battle over Worship

AT A WORSHIP SERVICE I ATTENDED A COUPLE OF YEARS AGO, my attention was drawn to the enthusiastic worship leader. He opened our time with prayer, asking God to meet us and draw us together in the Lord's presence. Then he turned around to face forward, standing just in front of the first row of worshipers with his eyes closed and the band playing. He lifted his hands and offered his joyful praise to God. That's when I really took notice, for as he sang so rapturously, he kept stepping all over the feet of the people behind him. Not just once or twice but repeatedly throughout the singing in the two-hour service, he kept "tromping in the spirit." No apology. No sign of acknowledgment. He was just praising God while oblivious to his neighbor.

This illustration metaphorically and practically depicts a significant part of our problem. I have no doubt the worship leader would say that what he was doing was unintentional. He was just so caught up in his own experience of worship that he lost track of others. In worship, he lost his neighbor. That's exactly the problem. For all of our apparent passion about God, in the end much of our worship seems to be mostly about us. We presume we can worship in a way that will find God but lose track of our neighbor. Yet it was this very pattern in Israel's worship life that brought God's judgment. Biblical worship that finds God will also find our neighbor.

What is ironic and especially pertinent is that many debates about worship are just indirect ways of talking about ourselves, not God. Our debates can readily devolve into little more than preference lists for how we like our worship served up each week. It's worship as consumption rather than offering; it's an expression of human taste—not a longing to reflect God's glory. Surely these concerns cannot be what matter most or are most at stake in worship.

When the disciples met Jesus, their world changed and enlarged. To call Jesus "Lord" and bow before him meant discovering that the world of God's compassion included the poor and the lame, the woman with the flow of blood, and the leper by the side of the road. If we worship Jesus Christ, then we are to live like Jesus Christ:

> Then [Jesus] said to them all, "If any want to become my followers, let them deny themselves and take up their cross daily and follow me. For those who want to save their life will lose it, and those who lose their life for my sake will save it." (Luke 9:23-24)

Just as such a response enlarged the hearts and minds of the disciples, this road of sacrificial worship is meant to do so in our lives too. In fact, Jesus says in Matthew 25:31-46 that our worship will be measured by how we have lived.

The crisis the church currently faces is that our individual and corporate worship do not produce the fruit of justice and righteousness that God seeks. This creates a crisis of faithfulness before God and a crisis of purpose before the world. Scripture indicates that our personal and communal worship are meant to shape our vision and fire our engines to be daring disciples, imitating and sharing the love of Jesus Christ in acts of righteousness and justice. What's more, the Bible teaches that the people of the world, whether they believe it or not, suffer and die while waiting for us in the church to live like the people of God, demonstrating our worship with our lives (Romans 8:18-25). The heart of the battle over worship is this: our worship practices are separated from our call to justice and, worse, foster the self-indulgent tendencies of our culture rather than nurturing the self-sacrificing life of the kingdom of God. We are asleep. Nothing is more important than for us to wake up and practice the dangerous act of worship, living God's call to justice.

Macro to Micro

I say this in part because I know that I do not stand outside of this sweeping critique, not for a moment. Nor do most Christians I know. Nor does the congregation I serve. Many of us in the church in the United States are simply busy with our daily lives. Apart from major headlines, few international needs go deep into our hearts. When we do pay attention, we often experience information overload and an unending sense of need and desperation when we hear of places like East Timor, Darfur, sub-Saharan Africa, Bangladesh, Haiti. We admit, in our benign lack of understanding, that people may be suffering in the world. But somewhere in our conscience we conclude that the suffering of "those people" is not what it would be for us; that dying of starvation in a refugee camp in Sudan is roughly the same kind of suffering experienced by the street person we encounter on the way to work; that it is utterly beyond our grasp to respond effectively to suffering on a global scale. Part of the malady of our culture and discipleship efforts is this tragic rationale: that in the face of global need, if we can't do everything, we can't do anything. We are paralyzed, inert.

I too am familiar with these feelings, despite my parents having raised me with a strong sense of public responsibility and social awareness. I remember going with them as a young boy to take food and other supplies to nearby camps of farm workers or to the villages of the Yakima Nation in Washington State. I remember them taking me to a dynamic African American church because they wanted to express their support of the civil rights movement of the time. Our family talked national and international politics and social policy at dinner as I was growing up.

When I came to faith in Christ early in my college days, the inner work of God's Spirit tended to be more apparent to me than the broader public implications of the gospel. Gradually life happened; my responsibilities grew, and a wife and children eventually came along. Preoccupation with myself, my world, my priorities, my church, my purposes were the typical order of the day. Sometimes this is overtly selfish, but often it's just that attending to such things is the natural default setting. Then, too, it is easy to become overwhelmed by the suffering and need around the globe. After all, who am I? What can I do? It is easy for us to think we should just get on with the relationships and tasks that are before us.

The gospel, however, has not left me there. Again and again I have experienced the compelling force of God's global compassion and attention. Part of what stunned and excited me when I came to faith in Christ was the discovery that if Jesus Christ was Lord, it mattered for all people everywhere. That meant God's heart was both personal and global. The kingdom of God was no small, myopic project but rather the transformation of everyone and everything. "For God so loved the world . . ."— that those who follow him are to do the same. This fit my background, but the gospel also challenged and deepened the call to engagement beyond anything I could have imagined.

Right after college I spent a year working and traveling, but the focus of that year was to get a clearer picture of God's work and presence around the world. My vision grew. My heart changed. I remember returning home one night after I taught a class on issues of world hunger at the church I was part of in Seattle. We had watched a World Vision video, one that I had already seen several times. As I was driving home that night, filled with a sense of the world's overwhelming need, I asked a question many of us have asked: why, in a world of so little, do I have so much? And I heard the Holy Spirit's plain answer: *In order to give what you have away.*

This was one of many important realignments in my life as a disciple.

I've had many such developments, but I approach the subject of this book as someone who is still learning; as someone who is rich by many standards, though I still don't feel that way; as a person, a disciple and a pastor who is still prone to live in relative inaction compared to the world's great need. Like others around me, I sometimes find myself busy with my worship, having lost track of my neighbor. And those are the good days.

Meanwhile our suffering world waits for signs of God on the earth, "with eager longing for the revealing of the children of God" (Romans 8:19). God's plan is that we, the church, are to be the primary evidence of God's presence. Every continent needs solid signs of that, especially in these times of extraordinary economic, medical, social, political and spiritual turmoil. Staggering statistics of land grabbing and bonded slavery, of malnutrition and starvation, of HIV/AIDS and wrongful imprisonment are rife. An enormous chasm exists between these daily realities of suffering in our world and the preoccupations of most Christian disciples in North America.

Jesus' call to "go and make disciples" must be carried out in a world such as this. The life-changing good news of God's saving love in Jesus Christ encompasses every dimension of our humanity and every aspect of God's re-creation of the world. Evangelism explains and calls people to respond to Jesus Christ, who wants to make every person and every thing (including every form of injustice and oppression) new. That is our hope and our commission as God's people. This holistic vision is the heart of God for the world. Our theology and our worship are meant to reflect that through lives that share God's heart for righteousness and justice.

First and Second Things

The core of a biblical theology of worship is the worthiness of God. Christian worship is only possible as our response to the glory, power and love of God as revealed most clearly in and through Jesus Christ.

The gift of God's revelation enables humanity to worship.

We can trust by faith, in clarity and in mystery, that the Word who was "in the beginning" has now been "made flesh, and dwelt among us, . . . full of grace and truth" (John 1:1, 14 KJV). Allowing the remembrance of God's revelation to shape daily life was a challenge for God's people throughout the Bible. At one point, the prophet Isaiah wants to help Israel recalibrate life in light of the God they worship and serve. Their tendency, like yours and mine, was for their vision of God to shrink. That's why Isaiah longs for Israel to recall once more the vision of God as he really is:

> Have you not known? Have you not heard?
> Has it not been told you from the beginning?
> Have you not understood from the foundations of the earth?
> It is he who sits above the circle of the earth,
> and its inhabitants are like grasshoppers;
> who stretches out the heavens like a curtain,
> and spreads them like a tent to live in;
> who brings princes to naught,
> and makes the rulers of the earth as nothing. . . .

> The LORD is the everlasting God,
> the Creator of the ends of the earth. (Isaiah 40:21-23, 28)

Worship is about this God and for this God. But our human tendency is for our vision of God to be small and petty rather than stretched to the heights and magnificence that he deserves.

One of the ways I practice remembering God's extraordinary love comes from living on the West Coast of the United States. By the time I wake at the start of the day or gather with my congregation in morning worship, the majority of the church around the world has done its work or finished its services for that day. I like to use this fact to meditate on the revolutions of the earth, thinking of the sun shining progressively on continents, communities, congregations, families and individuals. As I imagine this, I find it breathtaking to consider that God's loving gaze knows the whole and the part of every story and that he longs for life, justice and peace everywhere. When I travel, it enriches these images and intensifies my sense of awe as I ask with the psalmist, "What are human beings that you are mindful of them?" (Psalm 8:4).

To be centered on God means first discovering that God is our center and then living lives focused on the things that matter to God. We reflect the worthiness of God by how we love and serve whomever and whatever God considers to be of worth. This is how Jesus links the two greatest commandments to each other:

> The first [commandment] is, "Hear, O Israel: the Lord our God, the Lord is one; you shall love the Lord your God with all your heart, and with your all your soul, and with all your mind, and with all your strength." The second is this, "You shall love your neighbor as yourself." There is no other commandment greater than these. (Mark 12:29-31)

These commandments set the agenda for lifestyles of worship. No allegiance of love is ever to be greater than our allegiance to God. In God's being and purpose, these are not rival allegiances. Love for God comes first and leads us to love our neighbor. In fact, failing to love our neighbor throws serious doubt on whether we are loving God. So direct and serious is this link that the apostle John writes,

> Those who say, "I love God," and hate their brothers or sisters, are liars; for those who do not love a brother or sister whom they have seen, cannot love God whom they have not seen. The commandment we have from him is this: those who love God must love their brothers and sisters also. (1 John 4:20-21)

This comprehensive call to love God and neighbor is for all of God's people. We will either enact or undermine the purpose of our existence and our spiritual vocation by fulfilling this primary work God has given us. We love our neighbor by worshiping God and by encouraging our neighbor to worship God too. Our words and actions are meant to bear witness and carry that fruit into their lives, even as theirs is meant to do so in our lives. We see in the language of the prophets that faithful worship either does justice or risks being neither faithful nor worship. Let's see how it emerges in the narrative of Scripture.

The Story of Inseparable Loves

Human beings are created for God and for one another as stewards of God's world (Genesis 1 and 2). God holds humanity accountable for broken relationships with him (Genesis 3) and our neighbor (Genesis 6). The Lord considers the bad decisions and actions of humans to be enough of a problem to start over (Genesis 6), only to find that once again human power oppresses and injures even those within the family (Genesis 9). Despite their failure to love God and neighbor, human beings are given a fresh beginning when God eventually calls a people to be his own, those who are blessed to be a blessing (Genesis 12:2). Out of God's love for this people and their love for God will come an effluence of mercy and justice in the world: *shalom*. This common Hebrew word for greeting means "peace," but it also includes much more than that word typically calls to mind. Shalom includes our individual and collective well-being, our health, our safety and our completeness.

God later sees and empathizes with the unjust sufferings of Israel in Egypt (Exodus 1) and provides a way to freedom through the Red Sea (Exodus 2—16). During forty years in the desert, God's people struggle to see the wilderness, or each other, as God sees them. While Moses is on Mount Sinai receiving God's word for his people, they turn from worshiping Yahweh to worshiping an idol, and they turn on Moses, the man God called to lead them. A broken relationship with God leads to broken relationships with one another. God's purpose is to restore and heal both.

The Law is God's way, the Torah, and tells how faithfulness to God will lead to faithfulness toward one another and creation. It also defines and limits any and all claims of ownership and authority among God's people, affirming again and again God's compassion for the slave, the poor, the weak, the widow. No one is meant to suffer needlessly,[1] and God's people are meant to live that justice in reality. Here's an example:

> You shall not spread a false report. You shall not join hands with the wicked to act as a malicious witness. You shall not follow a majority in wrongdoing; when you bear witness in a lawsuit, you shall not side with the majority so as to pervert justice; nor shall you be partial to the poor in a lawsuit.
>
> When you come upon your enemy's ox or donkey going astray, you shall bring it back.
>
> When you see the donkey of one who hates you lying under its burden and you would hold back from setting it free, you must help to set it free.
>
> You shall not pervert the justice due to your poor in their lawsuits. Keep far from a false charge, and do not kill the innocent or those in the right, for I will not acquit the guilty. You shall take no bribe, for a bribe blinds the officials, and subverts the cause of those who are in the right. You shall not oppress a resident alien; you know the heart of an alien, for you were aliens in the land of Egypt. (Exodus 23:1-9)

No one is to be overlooked. God provides for Israel all along the way, and eventually the Promised Land becomes theirs, but not before lessons in redefining worship and neighbor, holiness and righteousness, power and powerlessness (Joshua). In the season of conquest, Israel gains the land yet often fails to distinguish itself as God's righteous and just people (Judges and 1 and 2 Kings).

God's call for Israel to remain separate is broken, their worship suffers, their social order decays, their values get mixed up with those of the
surrounding peoples, and justice is ignored. Even in the story of the
greatest of Israel's kings, David, we hear accounts of the profound ways
that failure to properly worship, by living God's law, resulted in indul-
gent disregard and failure to do justice. David rapes Bathsheba and has
her husband murdered, but when he confesses his sin to God he says, "I
know my transgressions, / and my sin is ever before me. / Against you,
you alone, have I sinned, / and done what is evil in your sight" (Psalm
51:3-4). David knew that wronging his neighbor was inseparable from
an offense against God.

David's reign may have been the peak of Israel's political life, but their
failure to live out their worship in ways that did justice becomes their
undoing. Through the line of prophets, God makes known that he is of-
fended: though Israel professes faith, they don't show it in their character
or actions (Amos 2:6-16, for example). God expects the lives of faithful
worshipers to demonstrate righteousness and justice. If they would have
done that, Israel would have been worshiping well. But in their failure
to do justice, they reveal their failure to worship. In fact, God says
through the mouth of his prophet Isaiah that in light of their failure to
do justice, it might have been better if they had not claimed to worship
at all:

> When you come to appear before me,
>   who asked this from your hand?
>   Trample my courts no more;
> bringing offerings is futile;
>   incense is an abomination to me.
> New moon and sabbath and calling of convocation—
>   I cannot endure solemn assemblies with iniquity.
> Your new moons and your appointed festivals

> my soul hates;
> they have become a burden to me,
> > I am weary of bearing them.
> When you stretch out your hands,
> > I will hide my eyes from you;
> Even though you make many prayers,
> > I will not listen;
> > your hands are full of blood.
> Wash yourselves; make yourselves clean;
> > remove the evil of your doings
> > from before my eyes;
> cease to do evil,
> > learn to do good;
> seek justice,
> > rescue the oppressed,
> defend the orphan,
> > plead for the widow. (Isaiah 1:12-17)

When God's judgment sends Israel into exile, they are meant to demonstrate in Babylon the distinctive character that flows from faithful worship of Yahweh: "Seek the welfare of the city . . . for in its welfare you will find your welfare" (Jeremiah 29:7). In other words, God says to Israel, demonstrate by your acts of justice and mercy that it is Yahweh you worship; live your worship in Babylon.

We find the same themes in the New Testament. Luke describes the inauguration of Jesus' public ministry:

> When he [Jesus] came to Nazareth, where he had been brought up, he went to the synagogue on the sabbath day, as was his custom. He stood up to read, and the scroll of the prophet Isaiah was given to him. He unrolled the scroll and found the place where it was written:

"The Spirit of the Lord is upon me,

    because he has anointed me to bring good news to the poor.

He has sent me to proclaim release to the captives

    and recovery of sight to the blind,

        to let the oppressed go free,

to proclaim the year of the Lord's favor."

And he rolled up the scroll, gave it back to the attendant, and sat down. The eyes of all in the synagogue were fixed on him. Then he began to say to them, "Today this scripture has been fulfilled in your hearing." All spoke well of him and were amazed at the gracious words that came from his mouth. (Luke 4:16-22)

Jesus does not distance himself from the themes of these two inseparable loves: love for God and for the neighbor, especially the poor and needy. He boldly makes them the centerpiece of his ministry. Jesus goes even further, emphasizing that Israel was so closed to God's purposes that God chose to give his blessing to the needy outside of Israel.

God's passion for the full spiritual and social renewal of God's people, through Jesus, is found throughout the Gospels (see Matthew 5—7; 25). It's also reflected in Jesus' poor reputation among the religious leaders because Jesus was a friend of sinners. His words and his actions drew the marginalized and the outcast. He loved the Father by loving those the Father loved. These cannot be separated. Jesus redefined the meaning of neighbor in the shocking story of the good Samaritan (Luke 10:25-37). Jesus shined light into the darkness of social stigma and alienation for Zacchaeus (Luke 19:1-10), for the leper (Matthew 8:1-4), for Matthew the tax collector (Matthew 9:9-13), for the woman at the well (John 4:1-43), for the woman caught in adultery (John 8:3-11), for the paralytic in Capernaum (Mark 2:1-12), and for the blind man by the pool of Siloam (John 9:1-12).

These were signs of faithful worship, for to love God means loving the neighbor in need. To those who fail to do this, like the Pharisees who "tithe mint, dill, and cummin, and have neglected the weightier matters of the law: justice and mercy and faith," Jesus said, "It is these you ought to have practiced without neglecting the others. . . . You strain out a gnat but swallow a camel!" (Matthew 23:23-24). Indeed.

The Broad Crisis

All of this shows that the real crisis over worship, in the history of the church and perhaps especially today, is this: will God's people wake up to worshiping God in such a way that we demonstrate we are awake by loving our neighbor in God's name? Will we demonstrate faithful worship of the living God—Father, Son and Holy Spirit—in which we are "to do justice, and to love kindness, / and to walk humbly with [our] God" (Micah 6:8)?

Every time we meet in corporate worship, whether in our Gothic sanctuaries, our industrial-park warehouses or wherever we gather to worship while violence, suffering and injustice don't miss a beat. Worship leaders especially may want to focus only on what seems culturally and socially immediate. But if we are coming to worship the Lord of all creation, the Savior of the world, then while we are setting up and checking the sound system or pondering prayers or sermons, we have to hold on to a wider vision of God's love, a set of very different circumstances and an outcome of our worship that is meant to land us in places of need.

For several years one of the gifts I received each Sunday morning was an e-mail from mission partners we supported who were serving at-risk children in Cambodia. This couple and their three small girls were living and serving among the poorest of the urban poor. In their humility, they knew the marks of this severe and demanding calling. One of the only e-mails I would read before the worship service was their weekly update. I read it as a spiritual discipline, as a morsel of mercy and truth, as a reminder and a call. I wanted and needed to lead our worship services in

Berkeley with my heart freshly reminded of the realities of suffering in the world, the urgency of hearing and living out the hope of the gospel, and the joyous and costly call of sacrificial living in the name of Christ.

Each Sunday I want to serve and be attentive to the people in the pews right in front of me and lead them into the transforming presence of God. The issue is, how can I measure whether this has been accomplished? What are the criteria? Scripture indicates that the answer will be whether those who feel blessed by worship live changed lives. The evidence is not just the immediate post-service buzz but whether people are actually giving their lives away for the poor and the oppressed in some tangible way.

One Sunday I was preaching on Psalm 27. It is a remarkable psalm of hope for God's deliverance from fear for those who have faced tough times. With the same candor found in many psalms, this one vividly describes being afraid and finding God's comfort. I'm sure it was at least a "nice sermon," maybe even a fairly good one. Later that week I attended a dinner sponsored by the International Justice Mission, a Christian human-rights organization that seeks justice for people facing various forms of oppression. Elisabeth, a beautiful seventeen-year-old Christian girl from Southeast Asia, spoke at the dinner. She had grown up in a strong Christian home, memorizing Bible verses, which became all the more poignant to her during the year she spent in forced prostitution, enslaved in a squalid brothel in a major Asian city. As she spoke, she projected a picture of her room in the brothel. Over the bed where she was so brutally treated she had written these words on the wall: "The LORD is my light and my salvation; whom shall I fear? The LORD is the stronghold of my life; of whom shall I be afraid?" These are the opening verses of Psalm 27.

I sat listening to Elisabeth's story of being forced into the sex trade when she was just sixteen years old. I thought back to the previous Sunday and my sermon on this same psalm, remembering some of the fears I had listed for those in my church. Those were real and legitimate fears, but none of them were as consequential as those Elisabeth faced. I had this image of a silent movie going through my mind—listening to Elisabeth while envisioning my congregation gathering for worship on a random Sunday. While we were busy trying to park our cars in Berkeley that morning, a task "so totally horrible," as one person said to me recently, girls like Elisabeth were coming to worship in their settings too. She came before God in her windowless room in the brothel. We did so in our glass-walled sanctuary. We were hoping the teenagers we sent off to the youth group actually got there. Once the car is parked, the teenagers are in the youth group, the band is warmed up, and the hour has come, what happens in our service has to have integrity, for the people in our church but also for Elisabeth. Somehow the God we name, the music we sing, the prayers we offer, and the Scripture we hear read and preached has to call us deeper into God's heart and deeper into the world for which Christ died.

Worship as Though the World Depends on It

If we see Elisabeth's story through the lens of the biblical narrative, we realize that love for God ties us to love for Elisabeth. Not because her story provokes some form of sentimental compassion, but because her life and circumstances make a claim on those who worship Jesus Christ. Our church's gathering together on Sunday morning and thinking about Psalm 27 is still God's grace seeking us in Berkeley. But in the midst of God assuring us that our fears are held by a God of infinite compassion and sufficient power, we must remember that Elisabeth's are as well. And worshiping the God who "so loved the world that he gave his only Son" (John 3:16) reminds us that we are to follow and imitate him for our sake, but also for Elisabeth's.

We are desperate for true worship that reclarifies the purposes of God and our part in them. When we stumble, "having no hope and without God in the world" (Ephesians 2:12), lost in false worship, the price for our lives and for others is high. False worship, which can be found as much among God's people as elsewhere, leads to distorted mission. Take power, for example. Power is one of the most profound gifts of God and therefore a prime target for false worship; that is, to take power and misuse it for something other than what honors God and his creation. Elisabeth's suffering, and much of our own, has to do with an abuse of power. Faithful worship helps us clarify and limit human power in our hearts and minds. False worship never does that. False worship sets the terms of injustice—a distortion or aberration of power. Faithful worship asks whether we are seeing and living in God's reality or in the fiction created by our own fallen lives. When we or anyone besides God assumes the central role, life whips us out of alignment—lots of motion with destructive wear and significant damage.

Layer upon layer of injustice and suffering, pride and entitlement, wreak havoc in our world. The fallout of false worship distorts our sense of God, ourselves and others. We justify our subsequent decisions based on this false premise, and the damage continues relentlessly. No wonder God gets angry at Israel—or the church—when this distortion is perpetuated by the very people he calls his own. This is the burning message of Isaiah, Jeremiah and Amos. This is a battle line in the worship wars that really matters to God. Whom do we fear?

Another distortion that false worship fosters is this: the loss of God's intended witness to love and justice. God intends that from true worship will flow lives that are the evidence of his just and righteous character in the world. False worship instead leads to false representation. We may speak in God's name but fail to show God's life. The prophet Isaiah says that when God's people do this, we lie about the God we represent (Isaiah 5:20-23; 29:13-16).

God intended for those in Abraham's line to be blessed to be a blessing (Genesis 18:18). Their relationship with God was for their own sake but also for the sake of those who through them (and us) were to "taste and see that the LORD is good" (Psalm 34:8). The world is meant to see and know something about God through the lives and actions of faithful worshipers. As we live out, carry forth, and demonstrate in character and action the life of the One we worship, they see God. "Everyone will know that you are my disciples, if you have love for one another" (John 13:35). False worship leads instead to a frustrated and often failed mission.

Worship That Reorders

Our context is breathtakingly different from the norm for millions and millions around the world. On a trip to India, for example, I remember talking to a pastor about books and reading. He said, "If I save for four months, I am able to buy one Christian book through a discount I am offered. I have never traveled outside India, but I have heard that sometimes people in America buy books and don't read them." He asked with dismay, "Is that really true?" I mumbled something to cover my embarrassment, as I thought of just such books on my shelves at home.

It's not a matter of *if* we have bought books we don't read, but how many. It's not whether we get our children's inoculations, but whether we can keep track of the paperwork to prove it to the schools. It's not whether we eat, but how much we eat beyond what we need or even want. It's not whether we have a bed, but what color and theme the bed coverings will be. It's not whether we have a chance to hear about the love of God in Jesus Christ, but which ministry or church or medium we like best.

Some people in our own country don't have these choices (a scandal in itself). But most people in America do. Meanwhile, millions in the Southern Hemisphere and in Asia have never lived a single day with choices like these.

This disparity between economics and justice is an issue of worship. According to the narrative of Scripture, the very heart of how we show and distinguish true worship from false worship is apparent in how we respond to the poor, the oppressed, the neglected and the forgotten. As of now, I do not see this theme troubling the waters of worship in the American church. But justice and mercy are not add-ons to worship, nor are they the consequences of worship. Justice and mercy are intrinsic to God and therefore intrinsic to the worship of God.

Where is the evidence that we are scandalized before God when we hunger for worship that almost never leads us to have a heart for the hungry? How can this disconnection exist and be sustained so easily when such incongruity is unimaginable to the God we are worshiping and following? Our worship should lead us to greater mercy. Our worship should lead us to costly acts of justice, especially for those who are the least seen, the least remembered, the least desired.

Vigorous biblical practice of worship should stop, or at least redirect, our endless consumerism, as our free choice to spend less in order to give away more. Our worship should be recognizable by the lives it produces, ones that plainly evidence the broad, sacrificial and persevering commitment of Jesus Christ. Our community reputation, as Scripture suggests, should be that the church comprises those who pursue justice for the poor and oppressed because that is what it means to be Christ's body in the world. We should not fool ourselves into thinking that it's enough to feel drawn to the heart of God without our lives showing the heart of God.

I experienced another of God's wake-up calls when talking with a friend who had recently visited South Africa. At the time, South Africa was still gripped by apartheid. My friend had gone there to see firsthand some of the worst parts of this cruel structure of injustice, and he vividly described to me some of what he saw. I was so overwhelmed by the layers of suffering he told of that I said, "It's all so complex!" He immediately replied, "Oh, it's not complex at all. Apartheid is evil. What's complex is how to dismantle it and bring about justice."

In that moment I woke up in an important way. The distinction between the diagnosis and the treatment shocked me. It was a plain truth. It pierced my comfort zone. I knew it made a claim on me if I wanted to follow Jesus Christ in the real world. In my sleepwalking life, far from Cape Town or Johannesburg, I was letting talk of complexity fall as a fog, creating a distance and a disconnection so I would not have to engage. What I sensed then and many times since is that true worship pierces that fog and shakes us into wakeful action. Worship reorders reality.

Scripture calls us to worship that affirms and demonstrates the right ordering of all of reality. Faithful worshipers kneel to receive and then enact the story of God's re-creation of all things. God's purpose is for us to "love the Lord your God with all your heart, and with all your soul, and with all your strength, and with all your mind," then go on to love "your neighbor as yourself" (Luke 10:27). This is God's right ordering of reality. By God's grace, what sin has distorted and injustice has dese-crated begins to reappear in the ordinary lives of God's faithful worship-ers and the world at large.

The stark track record of the contemporary American church, how-ever, seems to be that the plight of the poor and suffering have only a tertiary connection at best with our pursuit of worship. It is meant to have a primary place, as it does in the heart of God. That is the crux of the crisis. I and other Christians I know have been busy tithing the dill and cumin of worship forms while avoiding what Jesus calls the weight-ier matters of the Law: justice, mercy and faith. The perception that is-sues of worship and issues of justice are separate or sequential or easily distinguishable shows the inadequacy of our theology, both of worship and of justice.

Worship is to be the one activity that sums up the scope of our lives. We will explore in later chapters how faithful worship recontextualizes *where* we live and therefore *how* we live. The hope we are offered and are meant to offer others is that the gospel of Jesus Christ fundamentally al-ters the context in which we live. As we allow worship to do its transformative work in our lives, we can stay where we are and yet move into the places where the heart of God dwells.

We fight culture wars and worship wars over what we think matters. But the truth is, we get lost in our worship and step on the neighbor we have forgotten or ignored. We urgently need to recover a comprehensive vision of worship that recontextualizes our entire life and leads us to live out the worship God intends and desires. We need this for God's glory, for our transformation and for the mission of God in the world.

Worship means dwelling where God's heart is and showing it in lives that embody his loving righteousness and merciful justice. This is the worship war for which Christ died and rose. So why do we still sleep?

3 False Dangers

THOUGH GOD CALLS US TO THE DANGEROUS ACT OF WORSHIP, most churches like worship services that are safe. This is a source of our slumber and a symptom of our confusion. It reveals our instinctive efforts to manage the danger of encountering the living God. As a result, we give ourselves over to the wrong dangers and miss the real ones. As we will see, Shadrach, Meshach and Abednego didn't. As a consequence, their worship changed Nebuchadnezzar and Babylon.

When Safety Rules

A devotion to safe worship can be found across the board, from Low to High liturgical churches, from formal to informal, from traditional to emergent. In the best sense, safe worship encompasses positive dimensions that we call faithful, reliable, biblical. It can also include the safety of a rich theological or liturgical tradition, or of a meaningful spiritual style, or both. Safety can also describe the care taken to prepare a service that duly honors the eternal God and, by extension, the kind of substantial experience into which worshipers should be invited to participate. After all, in the Bible God gave spiritual, architectural, liturgical, sacramental and communal shape to public worship.[1] So far so good.

The problem with safe worship is not these strengths; they don't need to be forgotten or minimized in order to make a case for "unsafe" worship. Rather, the problem is that in the midst of appropriate safety lies the possibility and the common practice of domesticating God. There are a number of ways in our practice of corporate worship that we substitute human management and form for an encounter with the Spirit of God; we end up making worship in our image rather than God's.

Different churches have different ways of managing the experience of corporate worship. In traditional congregations, safe worship services are often one hour long and recognized by reliability, predictability and measuredness. Variation is kept to a minimum. For those who find even this low-level risk too high, sitting toward the back helps ease the stress, just in case something unexpected should happen up front. It's a study in control.

Highly "Spirit led" services can also become predictably safe. Such congregations have an orchestrated, unwritten but reliable spontaneity: who speaks, who doesn't; how the Spirit moves a specific person to bring a word from the Lord; the predictable sweat or tears; the expected flow and rhythm of emotion. Unlike liturgical churches, such charismatic congregations have a less obvious form of worship control.

Emergent services place control prominently in the hands of each worshiper, who might face a smorgasbord of worship stations and, based on their sense of themselves or God, assemble an experience they can affirm as authentic. The issue is still control; all that's changed is who has it.

The threat is that if safety becomes an overriding worship goal, we may miss the point of worship—encountering God and responding with our lives. When we have hold of form but miss substance, we may think we are doing something we really are not.

The Fear of the Lord

God's people should be the first to assert that "the fear of the LORD is the beginning of knowledge" (Proverbs 1:7). Here, *fear* principally means awe, not terror. The drive for safe worship services, however, usually squeezes out awe. Whether worship band or organ, formal or informal, it seems better to keep the awe manageable, the gaps minimal, the silence absent. This is changing for some congregations but is quite common in most, whether out of habit or production pressure to just keep things moving.

So much for encountering the God who spoke out of the chaos and called creation into existence. So much for bowing face-down before the God who spoke from the burning bush and from the whirlwind and from "a throne, high and lofty" (Isaiah 6:1). No, let's keep our assumptions and our structure safe. Three hymns or five choruses, two texts, some prayers and a sermon; out by noon, add coffee and it's just right! Or praise songs followed by more praise songs, spiced up with some candles and a video clip. Or worship stations and living moments. But, bottom line—modern, postmodern or emergent—just be sure it's earnest, dependable, reliable. Safe.

In the book of Daniel we read about Shadrach, Meshach and Abednego, Jews in exile in Babylon, facing the fiery heat of King Nebuchadnezzar's furnace. The king demanded that they bow down and worship the golden statue he had set up or be thrown into the fire. Shadrach, Meshach and Abednego had to distinguish between the lesser and the greater danger: fire or idolatry? The furnace was blazing hot, a dramatic threat. Idolatry by comparison was quiet, invisible, barely noticeable when everyone else was already on their knees.

The mesmerizing liturgical rhythms of harp, lyre and trigon sounded. All the three men needed to do was bow down. Yet their daily worship practices made it absolutely clear to these young Israelites that idolatry was by far the greater danger than the fire. So in the face of Nebuchadnezzar's rage-aholic tyranny, they responded to his threat with the simple words, "We have no need to present a defense to you in this matter" (Daniel 3:16). They were entirely unhooked from the life-threatening danger that the king was using to ensnare them. In comparison to idolatry, the fiery furnace was mere fire.

Mesmerizing practices are at the core of most cultural habits. But they can become routines that dull our sensitivities to real dangers. Just do what others tell us to. Don't ask questions. Defer any misgivings to someone else. It's like handing over our worship to someone else's responsibility. Worship is meant to educate us in distinguishing what is true from what is not, what is the greater danger and what is the lesser. But we often fail to exercise and strengthen those skills.

We need true worship to clarify true danger. We need to meet God in order to know what's worth fearing and what's not. When our experience of worship is committed to safety, it allows us to fear, even to bow down, before the wrong dangers. So the dangers of our lives are not being rewritten by the reality of God, as worship is meant to do. Rather, safe worship allows us to continue holding on to fear of the loss of lesser things, like personal status, satisfaction, power or happiness. Such worship leaves us with the same kind of blindness and confusion that grips our culture in general. How can we learn to love God and seek justice in a dangerous world in the name of Christ, if in our worship we have only experienced a domesticated God?

As a guest preacher I once assisted in serving communion following the sermon. As the pastor and I stood behind the communion table on the high stone chancel, the elders went up and down the stairs to receive the trays of each element. One of the elders lost his balance as he reached the top step and accidentally collided with another elder. Both silver trays crashed onto the stone steps, making the loudest reverberation at the quietest moment, communion bread tumbling all over the steps. It was a noisy, messy, awkward situation. It was also just an accident. But I saw such a look of fury and hatred pass between the two men as I have rarely seen. It was an embarrassing and painful exchange. The hatred was far more of an offense to that communion meal than the accident itself. For an instant it seemed the curtain was pulled back and I saw what our instincts often reveal: it's about us more than about someone else; it's about the lesser danger more than the greater one.

As pastors, worship leaders and worshipers, we bring the burdens and anxieties of our lives into corporate worship. From culture, social pressures, economic forecasts and life itself, we hear plenty of voices that give us reasons to fear: money, safety, health, terrorism, aging, parenting and much more. With each one comes corresponding notions of how to control it: work harder, exercise more, buy, connect, be cool, pursue what you want. Bow down before any of these, give them allegiance, and you won't get burned. But it's not true, and in worship God tells us so.

When the dot-com bubble burst, many people in my congregation were dramatically affected. One particularly successful dot-comer was truly broken by it. The flood of fawning messages that so many had given him over the previous five years about his brilliance, his creativity and his shrewdness was suddenly gone. The boom was now a bust. His life was shattered. *Fear* hardly seems to be an adequate word to capture the waves of anxiety and dread he was facing. Eventually he was ready to stand empty-handed before God. One day after I prayed with him he said, "The temptation is to run back into the burning house to save what isn't there. What I really need and what my life is really about never was there. I just didn't see that as clearly before now." He had been spiritually confused, but he came to see that he had bowed before an idol and hadn't even noticed "until [he] went into the sanctuary of God" (Psalm 73:17).

When so much is at stake in worship, we must confront the fear of being controlled by the wrong dangers. Only encountering the living God can lead us into the free life of the kingdom for which we were created, saved and commissioned in Christ. In this chapter we will look at some of the false dangers that shape our pursuit of safe worship. These underlying dangers help to keep us asleep, which in turn means we miss God and lose track of our neighbor. In the next chapter we will turn to some of the true dangers that set us on the course toward worship that transforms us and leads us to seek transformation in the world. If we are preoccupied with fiery furnaces, we will never encounter the hopeful danger of meeting, living and acting in the name of Jesus Christ.

False Danger #1: Worship That's Not Under Control

Whether mainline or evangelical, most churches tend to fear losing control in worship. Everything from the architecture to the highly trained clergy, from the liturgy (High- or Low-Church) to the music can be seen as control mechanisms. Of course, this could simply be an unintended consequence of what is put in place for different reasons (like appropriate decorum, orderliness, thoughtfulness). Yet the control message is very strong. Even in charismatic churches, statements like "You won't believe what happened in worship this morning!" are not common. Most Sundays we do know what happened because it is only what we expected. We planned it that way. We participated in it, knowing how it would all turn out. And it did.

As we have said, this approach may emerge out of a sense of tradition, commitment to beauty and elegance, or desire for healthy discipline. But the underbelly of these positive reasons is that human beings have always wanted worship to be under our control. We can trace this instinct to the beginning of time, when we see Adam and Eve wanting to do the only thing God prohibited. They wanted it their way, and so do we. It is part of our indefatigable and inflated sense of self-importance. We want worship our way.

This is partly behind the fear we feel about worship that's not under control, but what else is at play? Often we really don't want to meet God, or we fear that if we really tried to do so, we might not get what we expect. For some, this kind of historical, cultural anxiety comes from a latent fear of emotion in worship or of Pentecostalism or revivalism, or perhaps it is a cultural legacy of northern European culture. It may be a consequence of the professionalization of the clergy, who may "manage" worship because they think it's their job.

I became vividly aware of this false danger one Sunday morning in Berkeley. A pigeon got into our sanctuary. The ushers were trying to get it out before the start of the service, and at first I was helping them. But suddenly it dawned on me that this pigeon may be God's gift to us that morning. A pigeon flying around the church was funny yet made us feel somewhat uncomfortable. We didn't know where it would go, what it would do or where it would do it! The service was out of control, and it hadn't even started. As I greeted people that morning, I said that the pigeon was our call to worship. It put us on edge. The pigeon brought a sense of expectancy and watchfulness. I said that if we were holier God might have sent a dove. But since we're only Presbyterians, all we got was a pigeon! But worship was opened up for us by that uncontrollable pigeon. How much more are we to be open to the uncontrollable work of God's Spirit.

The breath of God's Spirit will blow with or without control. But our desire for controlled worship can hamper or quench the Spirit's freedom, and perhaps that is at the root of our intentions. The God of Scripture is not a God of disorder, but surely God's ways are not our ways, nor are God's thoughts our thoughts (Isaiah 55:9). Our Sunday services can become efforts to orchestrate intimacy without contact, to seek encounter without risk. The danger of losing control in our worship is an apparent danger to us but irrelevant to God.

Over the last several years our congregation has held special healing services as well as traditional services on holidays in the church year, such as Ash Wednesday, Maundy Thursday, Good Friday and others. By God's grace, we are open to new things—a good thing in Berkeley! These services have led us to some moving and wonderful experiences of having God in control of our worship. In them we have substantial periods of silence and a simple and provocative liturgy. Often we have some form of response. At one of our healing services, we had about fifteen minutes during which the only sound was the tearing of cloth, which symbolized the biblical practice of rending sackcloth. It was a stunning audio effect to accompany our common brokenness, anguish and lament. The subsequent silence was a profound and surprising grace. God met us there, and we knew it.

The trajectory of true worship places our lives under the control of God's Spirit. Some would argue that predictable worship is simply the church's administration of that responsibility. In fact, the fear of losing control in worship is the inversion of what should actually trouble us. If relinquishing control to God is what truly happens as we gather in worship, then it ought to be producing lives that are being transformed to look like God's life. Then, the more that our worship services lead us into lives of worship, the more we would demonstrate this by attending to the neglected, loving our enemies and remembering those in prison. But with all of our controlled worship, far too little of such evidence can be found. Our fear of losing control means bowing before the wrong god. Are we seeking to worship God or manage him?

One year when Christmas fell on a Sunday, my congregation arranged to hold a special service even though we don't normally gather on Christmas Day. We decided to have only one morning service and to invite everyone to this family service. As the church filled up, I was thrilled but a little anxious about part of the upcoming service—an open microphone opportunity. It had seemed like a good idea when we were unsure of attendance, but now it seemed like it might not work as well with the sanctuary overflowing. Each of the pastors sat on a stool in front of a large Christmas tree and shared something in our lives that we wanted to give Jesus in the coming year. Our words were honest, tender, unrehearsed. Then, with some trepidation, we proceeded to the next stage of the service, opening up the floor to anyone who might like to stand and share in the same way.

The first person to speak was a new father who said he wanted to give his tongue to Jesus because he realized that as a parent he would need to do that repeatedly over the years of parenting ahead of him. The next was a seven-year-old girl whose family was going through a very tender time. In the sweetest, most earnest voice she said, "The most important thing to me is my feelings. So I would like to give Jesus all my feelings because then I will have given him the best things I have." The next was a young teenager who said, "I want to give Jesus my time 'cause when I'm at church I'm all 'Yeah, God!' but when I get home I'm all Internet chat time." Next was another young man who said he wanted to give Jesus his attitude, especially toward his parents. In a matter of moments, the transforming power of the incarnation of Jesus Christ was seen in life-changing reality.

It was not "safe" to hand the microphone over to an unknown set of speakers. But if we hadn't taken this little risk, we would have missed encountering God in ways that surprised and moved us. Every dimension of worship that helps us grow in our capacity to trust God gives us the courage for the truly risky work of seeking justice in a dangerous world. If that's the trajectory, then we need to take every opportunity to meet and trust the One we follow. The point is not spontaneity per se. The point is worship that opens us to a genuine, transformative encounter with God, who is under no one's control. The Christmas service was one of those moments in communal worship that told us we are not alone and we are not the primary actors.

False Danger #2: Worship That Doesn't Seem Relevant

The pressure to be relevant is everywhere. One of the last things anyone in church leadership wants to be charged with is being out of touch. Yet isn't this just how the church is typically seen? So what do we attempt to do? Make sure that our services are relevant. The criteria for appropriate relevance include things like a contemporary service, a great sound system, projection screens for songs and images, video clips. We try to look, sound and feel like we are relevant, just like the broader culture. It's about technology. It's about speed. It's about volume. It's about now. Even the retro efforts of emergent worship take this to an extreme by making the worship experience about the relevant moment.

It's necessary, of course, to remember that the Christian faith is based on the central affirmation that God has come to humanity through Jesus Christ. The incarnation demonstrates personally and tangibly that God's love and his kingdom are the most relevant things in the universe. Incarnational ministry is the cornerstone of how the church is to carry out its life. This means that we seek to be relevant to those around us and to communicate this message clearly.

In doing so, however, we should be discerning about mimicking the culture rather than truly entering into it. We tend to make relevance a value in and of itself, and that may or may not be right in light of the gospel. Megachurches lead the way. On the one hand, they provide a positive example in their willingness to move away from traditional church models and toward models more familiar to unchurched people. But this leads to both good and bad news. The resources they have for staff and technology allow their cultural literacy to develop faster and more sophisticatedly. They set an example for other congregations who try to follow suit. They show "also-ran" congregations how to avoid being irrelevant. The primary message of many megachurches is that they will do almost anything to prove their relevance. They have been helpful in forcing churches of all sizes and shapes to rethink the paradigms of life and ministry that they have been following. So megachurches have helped reshape church life. But often such churches, or those who mimic them, are not mindful of the problematic assumptions they also may be promoting.

The positive side of this danger is that nothing could be more relevant than the God who made us and came to live among us in Jesus Christ. The real danger is not that we pursue relevance too much but too little:

it's too much about our culture and too little about God. So pastors, worship leaders and church ministries spend a great deal of time on Christian subcultural packaging that is intended to carry the gospel indistinguishably into secular culture. Christian music, memorabilia, books, media, conferences and so on look just like their non-Christian versions. When a new Christian television series called *Gifted* was developed in response to the popular *American Idol,* it was no great shock. Those who created the show explained, "It is our goal to wrap God's message—His love—in acceptance, and in a way that blends seamlessly into 'pop' culture while still upholding the values we, as Christians, value most."[2]

This type of relevance often means mimicry of human culture instead of the heart and passions of God. The church that gives in to the wrong kind of relevance runs the danger of losing its saltiness and finally having nothing to offer. The question of many secular people is not, "Why doesn't the church look more like us?" Rather, their perceptive question (and God's too) is, "Why doesn't the church look more like Jesus?" Safe worship never gets to this point. The risk is too high.

One day I was walking down Telegraph Avenue, the main street for students at the University of California in Berkeley. A young man who looked like a graduate student stopped me and introduced himself. He had a couple of prominent neck tattoos and buzzed hair. He said he had been at UC for a couple of years and had stumbled upon our church's worship services on his own. He explained that he was a skeptic, that he had no religious background and quite a lot of anti-Christian bias, politically and theologically. He had been a professional rock musician, dabbled in various religions, and now had returned to graduate school while he tried to figure out who he was and what he really wanted to do with his life. (This is just the sort of conversation that makes me love ministering in Berkeley.)

The young man told me that he couldn't connect with our contemporary services, but he could connect with the tone and style of our traditional services. He'd recently been asking himself some of life's biggest questions about truth, love and justice, and he was trying to find a church that would welcome him as well as his questions. He said, "I hate the 'Christian right' thing. Don't get me wrong—I think the world is going to hell too, but I think I'm supposed to do something about the places of real suffering. So far, the churches that match my politics haven't helped me with what I wonder about most: Is there really a God? Can we know if Jesus was God in human flesh? What difference would it make to follow Jesus?" He continued, "I think if I got clearer on some of that, I would know why my life matters and how I am supposed to live. I can find lots of people in this town that are like *me*. What I need instead is to find some people that are like Jesus. Is your church that kind of place?" He's right to ask, since surely that's the kind of relevance we need.

False Danger #3: Worship That Doesn't Meet Expectations

Among the many other things that churches are, they are an overflowing cornucopia of expectations that come from every angle, age, interest and demographic. Many churches do a juggling act around strategies for not upsetting people by failing to meet their expectations. After all, the people are the ones paying for it all. This false danger is concerned with dissent or tension, unease or conflict. The church functions as a way station for those who need less stress, not more. Simply put, the church exists to please people. Pastors fill their own need to people-please, and they measure the "unity of the Spirit in the bond of peace" (Ephesians 4:3) with customer satisfaction. This again is an apparent danger, but clearly not one that bothered Jesus.

In this framework, weekly worship becomes a kind of service center for those in attendance. It's about meeting their expectations, filling in their empty spaces, providing for their tastes, attracting their interest, keeping them coming back. The strategy is to provide a smorgasbord of hope. The more choices, the more popular. The more popular, the more consumer-believers are satisfied. The danger here is the anxiety of disappointing or upsetting the congregation. The question "How was worship today?" could refer to anything, from the singing to the sermon to good laughs to interesting announcements. More commonly the questions are, "Did you *like* worship today? Did you *like* the sermon today?" These questions are about human expectations and tastes, nothing more.

Besides the desire for tranquillity in the community, often the unstated practical anxiety is money. If people aren't satisfied, they might stop coming. If they stop coming, they stop giving. That jeopardizes everything. In a culture that's all about turning people on, we try not to do anything to turn them off—especially if it means losing their money.

In the meantime, the real danger of failing to meet God's expectations doesn't seem to arise.

Just a couple of years ago I was talking to an admired and popular pastor I know. He was describing changes he was making in the worship services at his church because he thought the people would feel it would better meet their needs. I understood what he meant, and didn't necessarily disagree with the changes. But when I mentioned that the key is to remember what worship means to God, not the church, he looked taken aback. I had at least expected a nod of agreement, but instead he said, "I don't remember ever thinking about what our worship means to God. I have only been concerned with what the church thinks of it."

The danger of failing to meet the expectations of God has been marginalized. This is not new for God. But by investing in safe worship that satisfies the people, we sell our birthright. We surrender the markers God has established as the distinctives of his people, the things that we are to be and do in the world as a consequence of worship that is only concerned about meeting God's expectations.

Worship that is based on people's expectations is typically shaped more by culture than by the gospel. The expectations emerge out of lives affected by consumerism, individualism, self-interest, entertainment, technology, class, race and generation, just to name a few. Sophisticated leaders learn to navigate these minefields. They sound like they are about following Christ, but the metamessage is that they are following culture.

The elaborate VBS I referred to earlier was a mirror of what the surrounding secular subculture would have expected in any highly reputed summer day-camp program. Months of planning and thousands of hours and dollars were spent to create the experience. The final product probably exceeded the expectations of the people. The layers of upper-class subculture, however, were so thick that to me the gospel seemed harder to hear, more difficult to access and more distasteful to live. I wondered if the VBS program would actually help the children and adults involved wake up to worship and justice, or actually anesthetize them. Most churches aim to meet the expectations of our people and subcultures. But where do we wrestle—whether saying yes or no to the subculture—to meet God's expectations for our worship?

False Danger #4: Worship That Isn't Popular

This danger is closely related to not meeting expectations, but it has an added twist. Popular worship services, whether traditional or contemporary, up the stakes of congregational approval by regularly surpassing expectations and becoming the place with "the buzz." This raises the bar of performance in one or more areas of the church's worship life. The buzz is often focused on a particular leader—a musician, a singer or a preacher. The hook in such worship services is a performance by someone who is the main factor in keeping people coming back.

Again, money lurks behind this danger, especially when a church has a track record of popular leadership. A whole church—its worship services and more—can readily be built on the assumption of continued popularity. Buildings, program, staff, vision—it can all be built on the back of a popular leader's ratings. The more this is leveraged for the sake of extending the church's ministry, the more of a hidden but controlling influence this danger has as it plays itself out for leader and congregation alike. Think of churches that have taken large risks to go forward with building efforts or television programming or advertising or staffing. Then suddenly a popular leader leaves, and the financial structure cannot be sustained.

Jesus' ministry drew large crowds, but that never determined what he said or did. Popularity that seeks to be safe inevitably panders to its followers: "Just give the people what they want!" But Jesus never did that. What he did drew attention to himself, sometimes for dramatic and spectacular reasons. But the expectations that he fulfilled were the Father's. The popularity Jesus sought was "Well done, good and faithful servant" (Matthew 25:23 RSV). This sort of pietism has seldom been popular. It's not safe to believe with courage, to speak with honesty, to love with humility or to serve with sacrifice. Safe worship that's defined by popularity runs the risk of fostering lives that never "grow up in every way into him who is the head, into Christ" (Ephesians 4:15).

The prophets and the apostles did not seek popularity. Their burden, however, was not safe worship. It was the danger of a living encounter with God, who wants to change his people and the world. God wants us to express the hunger that begs repeatedly for bread because it is so clear to us that our world lives with overwhelming need. The pursuit of popularity exists where the supply is rich enough to provide plenty of options, some more popular than others. But for a world that is starving for food of any kind, for food that truly satisfies, we need to realize that our fixation with popularity indicates how little we understand about our own hunger, let alone the hunger of the world. Starving people do not need popular food. They are dying for food that satisfies.

Justice is not popular. Mercy is not a hot topic. Neither one is going to be on the cover of *People* magazine. Neither is going to raise the ratings. Yet both absorb the heart of God.

False Danger #5: Worship That Isn't Comfortable

This danger assumes that most people come to church for comfort, which means we should do all we can to make them feel comfortable. That's an unfortunate correlation.

The danger of comfort calls for various strategies: regularity, rhythm, pleasantness. In a world where many feel assaulted by hassles and the real pain and suffering of contemporary life, being comfortable is important. No doubt we are better learners when the environment we are in helps us feel comfortably at home. No doubt when the physical and aesthetic aspects of a church are restful and adequate, we don't feel on guard or on edge. Most importantly, the Holy Spirit is the Comforter who comes alongside us and dwells in us to provide God's solace, healing and power.

In a post-9/11 world, in a context of economic, social, professional and ethical pressures and worries, people do need comfort. Our world is confused, scary, violent and capricious. Perhaps even the comfort food of baked-potato worship—corporate worship bent primarily on what is familiar and settling to our pressured lives—has its place. However, it keeps us from realizing and fully grasping that attaining comfort may mean facing pain, admitting wrong, confessing sin, showing weakness, admitting blindness, seeking healing. Names like Moses, David, Job, Zacchaeus, Peter and Matthew come to mind. For them and for us, the awkward, sometimes painful things we must face never tend to be comfortable. But they are a part of finding comfort. Meanwhile, giving people baked potatoes may make them comfortable in the short term. It may keep everything on an even keel, but it is for the sake of a comfort that can't be found in this way.

Traditional churches and seeker churches alike have made an art form of figuring out how to make unchurched people feel comfortable. The best intention of most churches is to show people the comfort of God's love in Christ. However, it ought to be of more than passing significance that comfort has not been high on God's methodology list. Wilderness? Exodus? Exile? Incarnation? Crucifixion? Taking up your cross? These elements of the biblical narrative suggest that God does not prize comfort.

Any ministry of hospitality, of welcome and community, can and should mean attending to the comfort of guests and newcomers. Meeting unchurched people where they are and understanding the expectations of inhospitability that many newcomers have about the church all makes sense. It is important to keep any unnecessary obstacles out of the way of unchurched people and to realize the deep, invisible thirst everyone has to be known and loved. All of that cries out for appropriate attention to comfort. But we must also admit that Jesus' strategy was to confront and challenge as often as to provide words of comfort. He healed the paralytic in Mark 2, but not till he had first said, "Son, your sins are forgiven"—not the comfort the paralytic had been seeking. Or when the rich man asked, "What must I do to inherit eternal life?" Jesus told him to sell everything and follow him (Mark 10:17-23).

"Safe worship" sees discomfort as a danger. It's disruptive. People don't like it. Do we really want to seek and encounter the God of heaven and earth? Too often we just want the padded pews, the call to giving that sounds challenging but doesn't have to be too sacrificial, the sermon that entertains and moves us without indicting us, services that are just long enough but not too long and great lattes when it's all over.

Hassled, harried people want comfortable worship. Services with silence, with gentle, restorative meditation and reflection are so important these days. People in my congregation in Berkeley, and many others, are hungry for longer and richer times of contemplation. But the implication can be that safety and comfort matter most. Doing justice, unfortunately, seldom feels comfortable. Yet that is the comfort God longs for the oppressed to know through the lives of those who worship in spirit and in truth.

False Danger #6: Worship That's Unfamiliar

This danger is about the fear of the unknown. Here we assume that worshipers mostly already know what they want to know—they just want to hear it again. Many don't venture into unexplored or untested territory. This is sometimes how tradition functions. It assures us with the familiar, but it can also box us in. It tells us that the familiar is what is good and right. The unfamiliar is neither needed nor wanted.

At one of the lowest points of my life, while in seminary but without an immediate church home, a friend asked me to attend his confirmation as an Episcopalian. I had been attending less formal churches, trying to find one that offered a trustworthy lifeline in this desperate time. All of them seemed to require that I encounter God through the worship leader, who was there to facilitate my encounter with God. The worship leaders were just a little (sometimes a lot) too enthusiastic and cheery in contrast to where I was emotionally. I was in a difficult place, and the personal, spontaneous worship style of these churches was leaving me emptier each week.

Then I went to my friend's confirmation. The service allowed me to fall onto the pallet of its profound liturgy and be carried by its substantial and stable affirmations into the healing presence of God. The familiarity of the liturgy in the mouths of the pastors and the congregation provided a power of transformation that nourished, renewed and encouraged me. It was through words that were not my own, that didn't come from those up in front or beside me, that I found my own voice in the wilderness. So I do not doubt that worship that is familiar has rich and substantial value.

Like all the other false dangers, some truth can be found in the fear of unfamiliar worship. The faithful practice of the gospel is not about what is new and improved, but about passing on "as of first importance" what has been received (1 Corinthians 15:3). Being faithful does mean valuing what has been revealed and rightly handling the treasure of that revelation. The hidden assumption, however, is that we already know, quite sufficiently, what has been revealed. Therefore we don't need or want what might be unfamiliar.

The unfamiliar spells danger. It might mean reexamining our faith. It might take us into areas of feeling that can be awkward, or it might disrupt the stasis of our community. The unfamiliar might mean having to cope with a more complex reality than we really want. It might cause us to be critical of where we have been and what we have believed or experienced. It is a danger because it can be alluring, yet it can realign things in ways that may be painful and disorienting. It violates the sense of being in control, safe. It leads to questions, redefinitions, new actions, different relationships. This is just what Abraham, Moses, David, Jeremiah, Isaiah, Amos, John the Baptist and Jesus each knew all too well.

When life seems overwhelming, the unfamiliar feels like encountering an alien more than a friend. For the sleeping, the unfamiliar can be another name for a nightmare. We have ways we like our coffee, our steak, our bed. We have ways we like to get up. We have our favorite television programs. We have our favorite moments in worship services too. We may like that a liturgical element is handled the same each time. We have favorite hymns that by their familiarity resound in our souls with profound meaning.

But the unfamiliar? Meeting the God whose thoughts are not our thoughts and whose ways are not our ways? Maybe under the right circumstances it can be tolerated as a temporary change, as long as the familiar returns and the unfamiliar is a short diversion. But please, no new habit of embracing the unfamiliar.

We don't want worship to be about what we don't know. It is a danger that makes us too uncomfortable. We really don't think that God is Other, most truly the Unfamiliar. We don't really want to cope with the different, the stranger and the alien. Never mind that God is Other or that the stranger and the alien are among those Jesus calls friends.

Safe worship. It's the kind of primrose path that draws us but misleads us. It has the allure of beauty but can mask pain, alienation, injustice. It can leave us feeling better but does nothing to help others who suffer. It can occupy so much energy and time that it leaves us too tired for ministry that might actually take us to where the needs are greatest. It can lead us to feel faith, but not actually to believe. It can lead us to imply we are trusting, without ever really taking a risk. It can preoccupy us with the false dangers of worship while we miss the real ones. It leaves us safe—which can mean lost, disengaged, disconnected, disinterested. So we often leave our services with what we came for, which sadly and ironically means we have little more than when we arrived. For better and worse, everything that matters is at stake in worship.

4 Real Dangers

WHY DO SHADRACH, MESHACH AND ABEDNEGO CHOOSE FIRE over idolatry? They know where the real danger lies. They understand that God brooks no rivals. It is better to die than to bow down before anyone or anything but Yahweh.

But that's not the way you and I usually see things. We don't realize that our beliefs and how those beliefs order our lives matter as much as the Bible suggests. So a few idols, if small and tasteful, tidy and not too obsessive, seem just fine. A little idolatry never hurt anyone, right?

Let's consider the biblical view of idolatry more carefully. God's prohibitions against idols first comes in Exodus 20, when God gives Israel the Ten Commandments. In the first commandments they are told to get this much straight: there is one God, and they must not worship any other god but him:

> Then God spoke all these words:
>
> I am the LORD your God, who brought you out of the land of Egypt, out of the house of slavery; you shall have no other gods before me.
>
> You shall not make for yourself an idol, whether in the form of anything that is in heaven above, or that is on the earth beneath, or that is in the water under the earth. You shall not bow down to them or worship them. (Exodus 20:1-5)

In biblical times, and even today in pagan and animistic religions, idols are the norm. Idols call forth obeisance and demand attention and various kinds of sacrifice. We in secularized North America may not worship the kind of cultish, godlike objects that are conjured in our minds by the word *idol,* so we might want to let ourselves off the hook. The truth is, our idols just look different but still demand obeisance and sacrifice.

The most popular idol in our culture is the idol of self. *I* am the center of things, and *I* try to make the world do obeisance and pay its price to me. This primary idol is virulent, autonomous and distinctly North American. It is more entitlement than arrogance or pride: I should get to feel, be and do what I want, when and how I want to do it. The idol of self can be broken into various constituent parts: my body, my abilities, my feelings, my choices, my perspective, my needs.

Also from this idol spring two other sets of idols: my people and my things. *My people* is the inner ring of those who are related by blood or who have been admitted into my circle by proving they deserve it and belong there. *My things* include all the stuff—material and immaterial— that establishes my sense of worth. These both can be idols, exacting a price that we are too often willing to pay with our lives.

We repeatedly idolize these things on a personal and cultural level. In microcosm, it seems harmless, or at least normal. We comfort ourselves by pointing to the ways other people are more extreme than we are. But these idolatries thrive. They extract allegiance from our hearts and threaten the true worship for which we were made. Repeated over and over again in the human heart and throughout humanity, these confused allegiances wreak pain and destruction, suffering and distortion.

Every time a church family gathers for worship, we come as idolaters or recovering idolaters. We all fight allegiances to someone or something other than God that make a claim on our lives. To pretend otherwise is to be naive and unprepared for the serious work of realignment we need.

One of the idols here in Berkeley is the idol of the mind. Every fall, Telegraph Avenue welcomes the start of another year at the University of California with special banners on the lampposts boasting the faces of all the Nobel laureates on the Cal faculty. Though the entering freshman class usually has a collective grade point average above 4.0, as well as long lists of personal achievements, Cal raises the bar higher still. The mind is one of the best of God's gifts and one of the most powerful potential idols. When our congregation gathers to worship God, we bring this idol too.

The challenge of cultural and personal idols is profound. Augustine described the crisis of human sin in all its forms as disordered love. Simply put, we are made to love God first and to love our neighbors as ourselves. In reality we love ourselves first. We are idol number one. Sometimes we love our neighbors, especially if they belong to *my people*. We either forget God or tell ourselves we don't know what it really means to love God. This produces the chaos we call normal life. This disorder lies within our individual lives and the systems of the world that cause so much of the suffering and injustice around us. We call it reality—it's the way things are. But Jesus sees the lostness this creates, and he weeps as he did over Jerusalem. It may be what is, but it is not what God intends.

God's saving grace to Shadrach, Meshach and Abednego came in the midst of Babylon, a place least likely to see Yahweh. In a foreign setting, these three exiles practiced lives of daily worship—the most life-changing and dangerously subversive thing they could do as strangers in a strange land. As we read in Daniel 1, they remembered by what they ate that though they lived in Nebuchadnezzar's house, they belonged to Yahweh. When everything that matters was at stake, their worship led them to live as God's faithful people in the midst of Babylon. It wasn't safe, but they embraced the danger of faithful worship.

Real Danger #1: Encountering God

Nothing is as dangerous as encountering the true and living God. Why? Because meeting God redefines everything we call normal and commands us to seek first his kingdom (Matthew 6:33). This is why God's messengers speak these words of assurance again and again in the Bible: "Fear not." The righteous, holy, all-powerful God, maker of heaven and earth, is no one's peer. "Is there any god besides me? / There is no other rock; I know not one" (Isaiah 44:8).

God cannot be tamed. God alone lives in perfect and uninhibited freedom. God is and will be God. There is no other. The witness of all who have had the closest and most personal encounters with God—from Abraham to Peter, from David to Paul, from Sarah to Mary—agree: encountering God means you will never be the same. This is the greatest (and best) danger of worship.

One day a man came to my office looking for help in making sense of the nightly conversations about Christianity he was having with his newly converted wife. He made it clear he was very busy, very successful and didn't really have much time for this—just some bullet points, now, please. It would have been easy for me to hand him some books or pamphlets. And while those can be good, instead I said, "I can see you are a busy and successful person, so I don't think what you're asking for is a good idea." Frustrated, he asked why. "Because," I explained, "if I were to give you some bullet points, and you were to really understand them, they would have such a significant way of working into your life that it could really mess things up. You would have to rethink the meaning of success, of time, of family, of everything really. I don't think you want to do that, do you?"

"No," he said.

"Exactly," I replied.

"Well, at least I don't think so," he stammered. "Maybe that's what we need to talk about first."

Christians confess that they would desire an encounter with God. But the church's avoidance of this kind of transformation, underscored by its avoidance of daring encounters with God, suggests that we choose to live something other than what we confess. We say we offer God our whole lives, but our practice (the evidence of worship that matters most) shows that we don't really want God to do what we ask—to take us, mold us, fill us, use us.

Over the years, I have had a lot of contact with parents of college students. For some Christian parents, sending their child off to Berkeley is a mixed blessing, a point of pride as well as anxiety. Many have prayed for years that their children would grow up to do God's will. Their children come to Berkeley, study hard, do well academically and grow significantly as Christian disciples. Ironically, though, when these highly gifted and well-educated sons or daughters decide to take their degrees and move into urban neighborhoods as servants of Jesus Christ or pursue long-term international missions as a vocation, some parents react with anything from anger to depression. They prayed for their children to follow Jesus Christ, but they really wanted that to happen in a mainstream, worldly successful professional life. They want it both ways. They say they want God to be Lord in their children's lives, but only as long as God leads in the ways they, as parents, want.

The same dichotomy exists in the midst of contemporary discussions and practices of worship. We change things, we say, in order to encounter God. But it easily dissolves into something far less. For example, many important developments are occurring in American churches, especially in our practices of community worship. Contemporary worship services, and more recently emergent worship, have been one of the most pervasive changes over the past decade or longer. The changes reflect a hunger for a more living spirituality, often measured by a deeper integration of our emotional lives with our experience of church and God. In the wake of the various worship emphases, the church has been left with "the worship wars." Not exactly an encouraging epithet! Battles over worship have turned us away from engaging God and toward simply arguing with each other.

We have been made for relationship with God. Therefore it is not surprising that we long to meet and know God. But the God we seek is the God we want, not the God who is. We fashion a god who blesses without obligation, who lets us feel his presence without living his life, who stands with us and never against us, who gives us what we want, when we want it. We worship a god of consumer satisfaction, hoping the talismans of guitars and candles or organs and liturgy will put us in touch with God as we want him to be.

The real danger of encountering the living God is like the difference between the gentle wind of our imaginations and the whirlwind of God's unmatched power and authority. Both involve air in motion, but the two experiences are in no way the same. Of course, God can meet us either way, or in some other way entirely, but what we need is to meet God. For that there is no management, no technique, no assurances of control. Without encountering God in worship, we easily forget doing justice and loving kindness, or if we remember, they become mere tasks rather than the very substance of life.

Ben was a very successful man. His professional life flourished. His family life was challenging, as a parent of several teenagers. For him, Christian faith was a distant and disconnected reality. But he began to have conversations about it with his wife and later with me. One Sunday I was surprised but pleased to see him in the worship service. As he approached me at the door afterward, his eyes began to fill with tears. He explained that while visiting Washington, D.C., for a professional conference, he had gone to visit the National Cathedral. He slipped into an empty side chapel and sat down for some quiet time and reflection. There, unexpected and unsought, God's Spirit simply came upon him. Ben became a new person. The awe and wonder of grace and truth beyond his own mind, his own questions, his own needs, simply met him and changed him. It was as though his life was utterly redefined, and it has been ever since.

Yahweh alone is God. He is mystery. Awe. Wonder. Glory. Power.

Love. Majesty. Instead of being awed by the incarnation, the divine concentrated in human form, we have allowed ourselves a presumptuous familiarity toward God. When God asks Job, "Where were you . . . ?" the point is to underscore the otherness of Yahweh. We are called to live with awe and reverence, "to walk humbly with [our] God" (Micah 6:8).

John Calvin proposed that God spoke "baby talk" for our sake.[1] Even so, it is the baby talk of the One who "in the beginning was the Word, and the Word was with God, and the Word was God" (John 1:1). Annie Dillard recognizes God's singular power when she writes,

> On the whole, I do not find Christians, outside of the catacombs, sufficiently sensible of conditions. Does anyone have the foggiest idea what sort of power we so blithely invoke? Or, as I suspect, does no one believe a word of it? The churches are children playing on the floor with their chemistry sets, making up a batch of TNT to kill a Sunday morning. It is madness to wear ladies' hats and straw hats and velvet hats to church; we should all be wearing crash helmets. Ushers should issue life preservers and signal flares; they should lash us to our pews. For the sleeping god may wake someday and take offense, or the waking god may draw us out to where we can never return.[2]

If we are committed to protecting who and what we are now, then our greatest need and greatest danger will be in meeting God. Of course, this is also our only hope. This is the wake-up call we may not want, but it alone leads us to new life. Becoming new will complicate our lives. Whether in the power of the whirlwind or in the still small voice of the Spirit, meeting God is no small incident.

God is engaged in nothing less than the re-creation of all things in the image of Jesus Christ (Colossians 1:13-20). God's people, through lives of worship, are to be chief instruments in that purpose. The world is to be renewed partly through the fruit of transformed lives that are righteous and just in character and action. The new creation is partly embodied by the extraordinary impact of worshipers whose changed lives leave a wake of love, mercy and justice.

To worship God with this trajectory is to take hold of the fifty-thousand-volt line of the Spirit's power in the world. It's definitely not safe. Each day is not about our needs and our schedules but about being drawn up into the glory of the One we seek to worship and follow. Our work is not just the day's labor but the way our heart, mind, soul and strength will be used to love God and our neighbor in the midst of our day's labor. As a consequence, we will realize that our neighbor is not just those who happen to live in the comfortable enclave of our own choosing, but also includes the needy, the suffering and the marginalized. For they are in God's heart, right where we now dwell. It's dangerous to let God shape our lives, for he always changes the neighborhood.

Susan finished her Ph.D. and secured a job in science education. She worked with kids, her first love, and brought all the passion, intelligence, humor and creativity she could to the task. But she kept feeling that following Jesus Christ meant taking greater risks. In time she decided to buy a home in a poor, mostly African American neighborhood in Berkeley, across the street from a park and a small community center. Slowly, faithfully, she built relationships with her neighbors, especially the children of one troubled family. She became a kind of surrogate mother for these kids, doing all she could to love and support them. Because of how she cared, one day the violence next door entered her own life when she was attacked by a neighbor's visitor. The physical and emotional trauma brought pain and confusion—all Susan had done was love the kids. After time had passed and the wounds had been addressed, it seemed that she would have to sell her house and move away.

Susan found a wonderful job opportunity near New York City. The week she left, she and I celebrated God's faithfulness through the deep challenges she had faced in her neighborhood and thanked him for opening this new chapter of his call on her life. Her first week in New York City was 9/11; the damage to Susan's block was so great, she was unable to live in her home for many months. Meanwhile, the gospel is still the same, and God's call for love, mercy and justice is still the redefining reality of her life. Six months ago as a single woman she adopted young twin boys from Ecuador. For Susan, it's just the overflow of bowing before Jesus Christ: "We love because [God] first loved us" (1 John 4:19).

Real Danger #2: Worship That Lies to God

According to the Bible, of the many qualities of worship that matter to God, none is more important than truth; that is, worshiping God as he truly is and showing that truly by how we live. From the opening chapters of Scripture, however, humans show a willingness to believe a lie about God and then to try and pass off the deception to God himself! From Genesis 3 onward, the human story is about the implications of that foolishness. Israel tries over and over again to tell God they are on his side, doing what he has commanded. But the prophets make it clear that it is a lie. The Old Testament prophet Amos writes of this. He starts with words of God's judgment on Israel's neighbors, but after condemning all their enemies, Amos speaks even more harshly to the lies and inconsistencies in Israel itself:

Thus says the LORD:
For three transgressions of Israel,
    and for four, I will not revoke the punishment;
because they sell the righteous for silver,
    and the needy for a pair of sandals—
they who trample the head of the poor into the dust of the earth,
    and push the afflicted out of the way;
father and son go in to the same girl,
    so that my holy name is profaned;

they lay themselves down beside every altar
    on garments taken in pledge;
and in the house of their God they drink
    wine bought with fines they imposed. (Amos 2:6-8)

When our protests of faithfulness are really sleights of hand, they anger and offend God. Saying one thing but doing another may work in our relationships with other people, but it never works with God. Hypocrisy is as high on God's hit list of sins as anything. The presumption that we can hide goes back to the Garden of Eden. It didn't work then. It doesn't work now. And blame—"The woman whom you gave to be with me . . ." (Genesis 3:12)—only adds fuel to the fire. God is no one's fool.

Jesus said, "Why do you call me 'Lord, Lord,' and do not do what I tell you?" (Luke 6:46). This is a contradiction that violates God's sense of being. Think how pervasively deception shapes human life. It is the air we breathe in so many contexts. It is not unique to any culture, though it varies in nuance and method. Lying has led the way in globalization!

The media and personal acquaintances give us plenty of examples, even within the church: sexual abuse by priests, graft by church officials, an elder who is involved in extramarital affairs, the college student who leads worship and goes home to cruise Internet porn sites. These are just a few of our garden-variety deceptions.

Only one community exists that has no history of lying: the triune communion of Father, Son and Holy Spirit. In the unity and diversity of God's being, only truth exists. The idea of the Father trying to pull one over on the Son or the Spirit misrepresenting the nature of the Son or the Son just plain lying about the Spirit has no possibility of truth. Naturally, then, God has fashioned us in freedom to choose to live in that truth and tell the truth—about God and everything else.

Of course, our finitude means falsehoods will sometimes come as a result of our human limitations. Assumptions that the earth is flat were ignorant, not immoral. But worship that lies to God is worship that willfully seeks to represent something that isn't true. In one of humanity's darkest hours, "the LORD saw that the wickedness of humankind was great in the earth, and that every inclination of the thoughts of their hearts was only evil continually" (Genesis 6:5). God will redeem that evil, defeat it and make it good. But now it is still evil.

Our central lie is in the discrepancy between the language of worship and the actions of worship. We confess "Jesus is Lord" (Romans 10:9) but only submit to the part of Christ's authority that fits our grand personal designs, doesn't cause pain, doesn't disrupt the American dream, doesn't draw us across ethnic or racial divisions, doesn't add the pressure of too much guilt, doesn't mean forgiving as we have been forgiven, doesn't ask for more than a check to show compassion. We "sing psalms and hymns and spiritual songs" (Ephesians 5:19) expressing our desire to know Jesus, but the Jesus we want to know is the sanitized Jesus that looks a lot like us when we think we are at our best. Despite God's Word to the contrary, we think we can say we love God and yet hate our neighbor, neglect the widow, forget the orphan, fail to visit the prisoner, ignore the oppressed. It's the sign of disordered love. When we do this, our worship becomes a lie to God.

Real Danger #3: Worship That Lies About God

This danger also causes God to burn with holy anger. Scripture indicates God has done much to reveal the integrity of his character and has called his people to demonstrate that character through living out his life in the world. The Lord hardly went to this labor to have the very people God has blessed to be a blessing (Genesis 12:2) distort the truth about him to themselves and their neighbors. The offering of our lives in word and action reflects the truth about God.

We lie about God by misnaming him when our lives and words attribute to God what is not his. That is, we claim to be Yahweh's people of the promise. But our failure to enact and demonstrate God's purposes with lives that do justice and mercy means that people attribute to God, or associate with God, the injustice, intemperance, impatience and self-interest of God's people. The watching world makes our weaknesses God's. That misnames God.

A recent national campaign to regain the cultural legitimacy of saying "Merry Christmas" threatened lawsuits against those who restricted or denied that freedom of expression. It was called an issue of free speech. That may be fair enough, but the real question is whether the church can actually demonstrate the presence of Immanuel, which is far more needed. The free speech issue clouds the church's attention to its real calling: to be the body of Christ. This more important reality would be clearer if, instead of boycotts and picket signs, millions of Christians chose to disconnect from a consumer-oriented Christmas and instead give that money away to those in dire need. In such an act, the incarnation would become more evident to the culture.

In another lie about God, we make the Lord of heaven and earth our tribal deity when we try to make him serve nationalistic ends. Whether we think of Constantine or the British Empire or American Manifest Destiny or more recent instances, religiously instigated nationalism diminishes God and subverts his mission. This is never how the Lord presents himself, but it is a frequent lie we tell others by our actions. We perpetuate this lie by making God out to be our nation's God, the One who has a preference toward us—deservedly, some say! God can be represented as the servant of our wishes, a vending-machine-type fulfiller of the desires of our hearts (Psalm 37:4), which are sometimes little more than Christmas lists.

In the Bible, God makes it abundantly clear that such deceptive worship is an utter abomination to him: "When you stretch out your hands, / I will hide my eyes from you; / even though you make many prayers, / I will not listen; / your hands are full of blood" (Isaiah 1:15). God knows when we are lying to him. But when we lie about him, our neighbor assumes we are telling the truth and determines that God isn't worthy of worship. We profess a God of love and mercy, but often the word on the street is that Christians who most insist on this are among the least charitable, the least forgiving, the most judgmental. In list upon list in the Bible, God describes the worship life of Israel—no shortage of activity, ceremony or leadership. It's regular, it's elaborate, it's intentional. And most often it's a lie.

When we "cease to do evil, / learn to do good, / seek justice, / rescue the oppressed, / defend the orphan, / plead for the widow" (Isaiah 1:16-17), our lives show forth the God we worship. We are meant to be God's clear signal to a watching world that there is a God who is the Light in our darkness. Instead we sometimes give evidence to the contrary. According to Isaiah, what angers Yahweh is the disconnection between worship practices that affirm God's love and mercy and lives that show it. This leaves Israel's neighbors in the dark. Through God's people they are left with a distorted vision of God.

Many outside the church suspect this dissonance, and some can even distinguish the difference between God and his people. Yet, instead of worship leading us into changed lives that change the world, we the church become one of the biggest reasons many people remain distant from and skeptical about God. It's a failure in worship that had radical consequences for Israel, and now for the church and our watching, groaning world.

Real Danger #4: Worship That Doesn't Change Us

If we truly meet God, we will never be the same. Yet in our worship practices, we have a tendency to stay the same. We go through the motions again and again, either failing to meet God or not prepared to let it affect us. We are like people who go through years of therapy because they seem to like the talking, but they do little of the work that fosters real change. Millions of American Christians spend hours in worship and yet lead lifestyles indistinguishable in priorities, values and practices from those in the broader culture.

To be fair, if human spiritual transformation were easy, it would not have required the cross, the resurrection or the gift of the Spirit. But these gifts have been given. They are ours in Christ. "Everything old has passed away; see, everything has become new!" (2 Corinthians 5:17). So why doesn't it seem that way?

Perhaps it has to do with incomplete worship. We take in the good news of the gospel again and again, but we fail to risk living out the gospel. Yet that is the necessary trajectory of worship. This is what James has in mind when he says that "faith without works is also dead" (James 2:26). He also writes:

> Be doers of the word, and not merely hearers who deceive them-selves. For if any are hearers of the word and not doers, they are like those who look at themselves in a mirror; for they look at themselves and, on going away, immediately forget what they were like. But those who look into the perfect law, the law of liberty, and persevere, being not hearers who forget but doers who act—they will be blessed in their doing. (James 1:22-25)

We are meant to live what we profess. If we are committed to disci-pleship that is defined by an hour a week (or more) "but do not have love," we are "a noisy gong or a clanging cymbal" (1 Corinthians 13:1). If we don't live the truth, reflect our praise or enact our confessions, our faith can't possibly change us.

Salvation has three tenses: we have been saved, we are being saved, and we will be saved. Christ's death and resurrection has accomplished our salvation in every tense. It's a fact of the past with relevance today and tomorrow. But we are also called to "work out [our] own salvation with fear and trembling" (Philippians 2:12) and to "be transformed by the renewing of [our] minds" (Romans 12:2). The clear assumption is that following Jesus will change our lives. We cannot earn our salvation by how we live, but we must show our salvation by how we live.

When we measure ourselves against those around us, we usually find enough evidence to convince ourselves we are doing well enough in the change arena. But Scripture's description of human change is profound transformation. We should compare ourselves to Jesus, not to our neighbor. That requires a great deal more change than we usually want!

Everything in Scripture points to spiritual transformation as our deepest and most profound human need. We share the universal need to be turned inside out (from being absorbed with ourselves to being absorbed with love for God and our neighbor) and right side up (from worshiping the creation to worshiping the Creator). This transformation is the most difficult thing in the world. Why else would it require the death of God's only Son? It is the highest price for the most costly and difficult change. So when we talk about spiritual transformation—being remade into the image of Jesus Christ—let's remember that it is profound and costly, that it required death for there to be life.

We should remember too that the transformation God seeks and offers through Jesus Christ is as extensive as it is intensive; it includes the re-creation of all things. Human transformation is a primary result within the wider cosmic work that God won through the cross and resurrection. Scripture assures us that this intensive and extensive transformation can be counted on and will be completed. The Bible also says it is not yet done.

The danger for us is that we might lose control, and we might not feel safe. We might have to face and engage the mess in our lives and in the world. We are right.

When we choose to worship lesser gods, giving ourselves to the same goals and values as everyone around us, we show our failure to worship the only One who deserves it. In this vortex of cultural conformity, God's people should be the ones to receive and give in worship all that we are and have. Only then can we be gradually remade into the likeness of Jesus Christ and become God's agents of change in the world. It's dangerous to take the gospel this seriously.

Real Danger #5: Worship That Doesn't Change the World

What is God's response to the problem of evil? The love of the Father through the Son by the Spirit. And how do the people of God embody that love and justice? By finding their lives in God through worship. And how is that reality to be seen and known today? By the people of God living and sharing their worship in lives that "do justice, . . . love kindness, and . . . walk humbly with [our] God" (Micah 6:8).

The sanctuary of our church has clear glass walls. At the time it was built in the early 1970s, every bank in that part of Berkeley had already bricked up its windows for protection against anti-Vietnam war demonstrations. The beloved old stone sanctuary had to be taken down because it had been condemned for seismic safety, and the membership of the church suffered through frequent riots, including one month in the 1960s when you could only get to church through the arms of the National Guard after Governor Ronald Reagan declared martial law on Berkeley. It was in that world that the congregation I am privileged to serve chose to stay on its corner and build a glass-walled sanctuary. We want the world that passes by to see us; but even more, we want to see them.

Almost every Sunday I envision in my mind's eye a group of protesters facing us as we worship with a sign that has this question: How dare you? The question captures for me the skepticism that always swirls around us. It also shows that people are watching what we say and do. We must respond, and this actually points us toward God's call. For if imaginary protestors ask this question, how much more does God? And our response is given daily in our individual and collective lives. It has to do with the grace of God that calls us to be recipients and agents of change in the world. We should worship and show it in our lives, for in doing so we share in God's reordering of the universe.

Imagine how shocking it would be if the foremost reputation of the church was "the people who endlessly love" or "the people who sacrificially put others first" or "the ones who always remember the poor and the forgotten." The point is not the accolades but living the life that embodies our true identity, the life of the One we worship.

The broad, cross-cultural appetite for such a witness is strong. For example, we saw global grief and respect following the deaths of Mother Teresa and Pope John Paul II. Of all that was said of these two people, their love for the needy and marginalized was the most frequently and commonly talked about, both by those who shared and disliked their beliefs. Why? Because they loved Jesus, and they sought to love those Jesus loved. Their worship changed them, and it changed the world.

In the documentary movie *Mother Teresa,* a priest who had known Teresa from her early days as a nun says, "People say Mother Teresa went to Calcutta and was moved by the plight of all those in need and felt called to respond. That was not it! She knew the love of Jesus, and it was specifically because of that love that she responded as she did." Worship changed her, and the consequence changed the world.

Why does a correspondence between worship and justice seem to be lacking in the church overall? Or in the American church? Of course, there are exceptions to be found in some congregations. But for the most part, the white, Anglo-Saxon, Protestant American church has such staggering resources, with so much freedom and so many opportunities to respond to the world's needs, and yet does so much less than it could. And this includes millions of people who often sing, "All hail the power of Jesus' name, let angels prostrate fall." The church in the safest nation in the world so often clings to its obsession with safety rather than risks investing in the cause of Christ in the world. That can only occur, however, if we awake to new life.

5 Waking Up to Where We Live

AS WORSHIP WAKES US UP, WE ARE IN FOR A SURPRISE: though we live in the same dwelling, God changes our address. By God's grace, the reference points that position our lives in relation to others are altered. The neighborhood may seem the same, but in time we will discover it is both different and larger than we ever imagined.

Location, Location, Location

I recently chatted with a stranger in a grocery store checkout line. He lamented how tired he was and how hard he had been working. He told me about the constant travel involved in his job and how it made things difficult for him. Then, a little self-conscious of his complaining, he said, "Oh well, I guess things could be worse." An enormous earthquake in Pakistan was all over the headlines of the newspapers around us at the checkout counter, so I said, "Yes—we could be living in Pakistan right now." The man's instant retort was, "Oh, I would never be that stupid!"

The comment was shocking yet revealing. Since I didn't know the man at all, I can't know exactly what he meant. But what struck me on the surface was the range of his apparent assumptions: (a) where people live is a matter of choice; (b) everyone is free to make "smart" choices about where we live; (c) it would be stupid to choose to live in a place of suffering. This man's comments capture the warp and woof of how many in America see themselves in relation to a staggeringly needy world: "They live over there. I don't. Their reality is not my reality. I don't want to know or share their reality. I am blessed. I would think they would want to be blessed too. I guess they are just stupid or stuck in their circumstances. Too bad. That's why they suffer, I guess. I sure wouldn't choose that."

With American culture as our starting point, we easily presume that what is true for middle-class life is true for others elsewhere—where millions of our brothers and sisters in Christ go hungry. Their reality is not our reality. We just consider ourselves lucky because we don't live where they do. To that, I believe Jesus would say, "Precisely—and that's the problem. If you worship me, you find your life in me and you live where I do. Those who are starving or in prison or oppressed are in my heart, just as you are in my heart. The victims of injustice and suffering are not only your neighbors, they are your family. Where they live, I live. Where I live, you live. So where they live, you live—in me."

The disjunction between our worship and the practice of seeking justice reveals a confused and impoverished understanding of where we live. Our readiness to live in Christ (for our sake), while largely ignoring our neighbor (also for our sake), shows again our failure to wake up to our new location. Christ's disciples are to worship and to show they do so by dwelling in God's mercy and justice. Our lifestyle of worship is to be lived out in the real world.

Of course, where we live does shape how we live. That is as much a fact for people in Pakistan as it is for people in the United States. Certainly the man in the grocery store line was telling me where he lived: in an individualistic, middle-class, self-assertive, autonomous culture. We all live embedded in cultural, political, economic, racial and geographic dwellings. But one of the great surprises of the gospel is that God sees our dwelling places with such compassion as to enter into them (the incarnation) and with such power as to transform them (through the cross and resurrection).

The gospel recontextualizes where we live. Knowing that where we live matters, God provides the good news of Jesus Christ to change our address. We didn't choose it; we were chosen. We didn't love God, but he loved us. Once we were strangers; now we are friends. Once we were far off; now we have been brought near. Once we had not received mercy; now we have received mercy (see 1 Peter 2). Everything is different. In worship, we practice living in the same dwelling while discovering our new address means we have new neighbors, a new love and a new calling.

The Personal Love of God

By contrast, "God the Personal Shopper" is too often the American Christian's projection of individualistic consumer culture, which creates a theology of self-absorption. Unfortunately, this consumer theology is too often what gets affirmed and practiced in our weekly worship or personal devotions. It's what allows us to keep sleeping in a faith more absorbed with ourselves than with God or the passion of God for the world. We need our life to be reordered by the far greater and no less personal love of the God who loved the whole world. The true love of God the Father knows every hair on our head. That is an expression of the greatness and expansiveness of God's love.

The personal love of God is like an equation that works one way better than the other: God loves the whole world, and that encompasses loving us individually. He doesn't love us individually until he ends up loving everyone. The difference is significant because the second order shows the influence of our individualistic American subculture instead of the God who made heaven and earth. If we think the personal love of God is the issue of primary importance, then we are more likely to try to make God in our image. We must see reality God's way rather than try to make God see reality our way. Many years ago J. B. Phillips wrote the book *Your God Is Too Small*. That title still captures one of our biggest temptations.

Yahweh's love for Israel was not cuddly. It was tender, personal, persistent, faithful and profound. Israel received the revelation of God's name, but they did not presume to use it. In love Yahweh drew near to Israel, for he was their God and they were his people. It was a bedrock love demonstrated in God's personal faithfulness. At the same time it was the love of the God who set the stars in their places. When Israel remembered both dimensions, they were in the right frame of mind.

Cameron came to faith in Christ out of a belligerently anti-Christian home. His father had raised him to be a rationalist. As Cameron grew as a Christian, the world became larger and more multidimensional than his father's rationalism ever allowed. His neighborhood grew, and so did his response to its needs.

When Elaine became a follower of Jesus, she discovered that the years of self-protectiveness she had used to keep everyone away began to be redefined. People she would not have deigned to talk with before became some of her closest friends. She had been groomed by her family to be an elitist, but in following Christ Elaine became a teacher in an inner-city school.

Juan had spent the majority of his life within the confines of his own ethnic group. His neighbors, school, activities and job were almost entirely with people of the same ethnicity. When he came to faith in Christ as a young father, Juan began to take steps into a much wider world. The church he joined was multiethnic and sent him into the rest of his world in new ways.

Think back to the story of Elisabeth, the young girl trapped in the sex slave industry in Asia. When International Justice Mission investigators showed up at the brothel and secured her safe release, along with fourteen other girls, they were embodying the love that is the Father's heart. Their actions bore tangible witness to their words: "Elisabeth, God loves you." Their efforts at follow-up and after-care for Elisabeth and the other girls continue to validate their confession of God's love. The IJM staff knows that "we love because [God] first loved us" (1 John 4:19).

Our call to worship means we still live in the same world, but we understand it differently. We still go to the same school or job, but we see it in a new way. We still function within the same culture, but the windows and doors are thrown open so we see what we didn't before. Through worship, we are to engage in a Christ-centered, refocused life and to live it out in dedication to the passions and purposes of God. The new address we have by following Jesus Christ has redefined everything about our context. It is now recast in the light of the larger and deeper context of the gospel.

In this gospel setting, we know that we now live in God's grace to share his love and justice with our world. This is not easy to do, but it is clear according to Scripture. Paul, in the benediction of one of his letters, sends us out to live wakeful lives: "Now to [God] who is able to do exceedingly abundantly above all that we ask or think, . . . to Him be glory in the church by Christ Jesus to all generations, forever and ever" (Ephesians 3:20-21 NKJV). In other words, "Now get out of here, go and live this out wherever you go. Realize who you are, practice where you live, and let it show in all the great and small ways God gives you!"

Sleeping In at Our New Address

But as we have said, we've got a problem: we can be asleep even if we are now living at our new address. And waking up can be difficult, especially at times when sleep seems so much more attractive than being awake—like when sleep is an act of avoidance.

This reminds me of how I've felt when struggling to wake up from general anesthesia after surgery. On the one hand, I remember feeling an incredible longing to be awake, to know how the surgery went, to regain my bearings and so on. On the other hand, I also recall feeling a disorienting force that seemed to hold me back, keeping me from accomplishing this goal. I felt like my brain was full of tapioca, and I wanted to be free of the sticky goop so my mind would work again. However, my body needed rest to recover from the surgery, and I felt like I could and maybe would sleep forever! I wanted yet didn't want to be awake. The chemicals in my body pulled me toward and also away from wakefulness.

This seems like Paul's argument in Romans 7: what I want to do, I don't do, and what I don't want to do, I do (Romans 7:14-20). The parallel is strong, and the battle is central to our discipleship: will we or won't we truly wake up to the purposes and life for which we have been called? As the apostle Paul brings his dilemma into full focus he says,

> So I find it to be a law that when I want to do what is good, evil lies close at hand. For I delight in the law of God in my inmost self, but I see in my members another law at war with the law of my mind, making me captive to the law of sin that dwells in my members. Wretched man that I am! Who will rescue me from this body of death? Thanks be to God through Jesus Christ our Lord! (Romans 7:21-25)

Worship leaves us with an impression that we live in one place. Our culture leaves us with an impression that we live in another. The crisis of our slumber leaves us with the impression that we still live somewhere that we do not. The tension between our two worlds can be awkward and painful. Meanwhile, where we *think* we live shapes how we live. We end up acting in ways that, from God's point of view, are grave distortions of reality. It's a bit like living out the story of *The Emperor's New Clothes*.

The Context of All Contexts

To follow Jesus Christ means to "put on the Lord Jesus Christ" (Romans 13:14), to be made alive after being dead (Ephesians 2:1-10), to be "born from above" (John 3:3), to "live your life in a manner worthy of the gospel of Christ" (Philippians 1:27). This new context for life, "rooted and grounded in love" (Ephesians 3:17), stimulates us to an abundant life, awake and alive in dimensions we might not otherwise have known existed. We are adopted by the Father and through the Son into the life that is now ours in Christ. As Paul put it, "living is Christ and dying is gain" (Philippians 1:21). We are to live the life of God in Christ through the power of the Holy Spirit. The Bible makes it clear that this is what leads us to matters of justice, for it flows from the very heart of God. It turns out God's heart is right where we now live!

The God who said "Let there be light" (Genesis 1:3) is the context for all of life. God's life could not be closer or more fundamental to us. The life of God explains why we live and how we exist. Whatever a person may think about God, all life comes from and is sustained by God's own being. We may or may not believe in oxygen, but it sustains life. So it is with God.

Before redwood trees and blue seas, before time and culture, before bodies and minds, before suffering and injustice, God is. "In the beginning God . . ." (Genesis 1:1 NIV). The fourth word is the most telling. Everything else flows from God. What's more, the Bible's first reference to God is not to a principle of the universe nor to an idea, but to One who speaks and acts. No prologue is offered. No cause or motivation is presented. God speaks, and his words perform and accomplish the act.

God's creative word provides the materials in and through which all things, including human beings, come to exist and to know and experience life. In contrast to the deities of other ancient creation stories, God is distinct from the world he fashions yet remains close to it. God is willingly dirtied with the material world, fashioning, molding and breathing life into those who bear his image. And he pronounces the world "very good" (Genesis 1:31).

In such a context, worship is life and life is worship. It is one holistic reality in consonance with God. Before we take our first breath or hunger for our first meal or read our first word, God was, is and always shall be; our lives seamlessly reflect this fact. God attends to us fully: "Even before a word is on [our] tongue, / O LORD, you know it completely" (Psalm 139:4). We have been "fearfully and wonderfully made" (Psalm 139:14), and we live in the presence of our loving, creative, attentive God every moment of every day. This communion is to be our primary home.

We live in a world where love is bartered, exchanged for roughly equal amounts between people of roughly equal means. The man in the checkout line knew this intuitively. So he said don't be stupid and suffer. This is why Scripture says our hearts need to be planted deep in the love of God so that we might know how far and wide and deep and high his love is:

> I bow my knees before the Father, from whom every family in heaven and on earth takes its name. I pray that, according to the riches of his glory, he may grant that you may be strengthened in your inner being with power through his Spirit, and that Christ may dwell in your hearts through faith, as you are being rooted and grounded in love. I pray that you may have the power to comprehend, with all the saints, what is the breadth and length and height and depth, and to know the love of Christ that surpasses knowledge, so that you may be filled with all the fullness of God. (Ephesians 3:14-19)

This text is not meant to be a tease, laying before us a love we will never know. Instead it depicts the very love in which we are meant to dwell, although it takes time to know maturely.

I try to begin each day by meditating on this affirmation of whose I am and where I live. I know it is all too easy to get caught up in thinking about the coming day—the activities, the people, the worries and the joys. What I want to do instead is take all those details and wrap them up in the greatest spiritual reality, that Jesus rules in love over all. I, and all those I will encounter, along with everyone and everything, are held in the heart of God. As a disciple of Jesus Christ, I don't just live at 20

Keefer Court. I live *in Christ* at 20 Keefer Court. That makes a world of difference as I live each day.

Today, for example, I picked up the paper and read about the ongoing tragedy of civil war in the Congo, where millions have suffered and died over the last decade. Now there is an effort to find someone to blame for all the suffering. Many are being wrongly accused. Twenty thousand children in Kinshasa alone, from toddlers to teens, have been accused of being witches. Because such children are often AIDS orphans, they get blamed for causing the death of their parents. The punishment they endure frequently involves public humiliation and torture by self-appointed "pastors" who believe they are exorcising these young children of evil spirits.[1]

Just think how many times this and other forms of perverse worship radically distort human existence, even that of children, who are the weakest. Though the situation in the Congo is an especially dramatic example, it is neither the worst nor uncommon. Being recontextualized in Christ means gaining a fundamental clarity and purpose that puts such tragic distortions on our hearts and minds, then causes us to show by our lives that such lies and injuries are intolerable and unacceptable. I cannot be in Christ and forget my neighbor.

Living in Our Spiritual Habitat

Out of love God gives us a vast creation in which to live and work, love and play. We are given the gift of human communion, since it is not good that we be alone (Genesis 2). The context of human life is to be communion with God, one another and the world in which we are honored to live as God's stewards. But that is not the choice Adam and Eve made or that we make. We recast our relation to God, thereby changing what it means to be human. As God indicated, we were meant for life but chose death.

Our self-serving response to God alters everything. This tragic legacy is replayed generation by generation as human beings live out of a distorted context, in havoc, blindness, deception, loneliness, confusion and injustice. This is the core of our human crisis. Yet God has not left us for an instant. We feel we have "no hope and [are] without God in the world" (Ephesians 2:12). We can't and won't bear that, so we devise means for remaking and filling our context with portraits and images of gods, while we forget, neglect, ignore or deny the context of the One who is and always shall be.

This vision of God and his relation to humanity includes, of course, the person who lives on the other side of the globe and the one on the other side of the tracks. Whether in a Hong Kong high-rise or an African hut, an American penthouse or an urban tenement; whether high-caste or untouchable, man or woman, adult or child, we all live and move and have our being from the God who sustains us by his very breath.

But there is more that God extends to us. God's solution is stunning. God's plan of salvation is to reestablish and recontextualize our lives entirely. Corporate worship is the language of God's re-creation. We are meant to wake up through worship to realize and enact where we now live by God's astounding grace. Not only does this new dwelling place in Christ *not* take us "out of the world," but rather deliberately and purposely, it sends us "into the world" (John 17:15, 18).

The Big Move

The life, death and resurrection of Jesus Christ changes the context of our human condition. By Christ's work, we are restored in our relationship with God, adopted into the family of God's people, sharing in divine communion. Grace reverses our pattern of moving away from God and welcomes us back. By adoption, we no longer simply live in the world with God, but by grace now dwell in God—Father, Son and Holy Spirit. The Trinity is not just an idea for us; it is our home. This is life's greatest wake-up call.

The biblical narrative unfolds gradually until we understand that the humble, mutually loving, honoring and serving communion of the tri-une God is our home. For this communion we are made. By this communion we are saved. Into this communion we are adopted. Out from this communion we are meant to live and serve. We are called to find our life as we dwell in God in the world. We live in God with our circumstances rather than living in our circumstances with God.

Ben Weir, a Presbyterian missionary in Lebanon, was suddenly taken captive on the street near his home in Beirut. He was stuffed into the trunk of a car and driven away, the start of what would be more than sixteen months of captivity. When he awoke the next morning, he was blindfolded and chained to a radiator in what seemed to be a very small room. Ben began to do something he repeated often in those days—he practiced remembering who he was. He would say to himself, "I am the same person, child and missionary of the same God, husband of the same wife, father to the same children, professor to the same students." He would remind himself, "I am the same person I was yesterday. I was not a captive then. Today I am. But that's the only thing that's different." The circumstances of Ben's life had radically changed, but his life was still in Christ, just as it had been the day before. He was living in God in captivity. For Ben, this is what shaped his whole experience of being held hostage.

In John's Gospel, we hear the language of the Son in relation to the Father. Jesus says, "Do you not believe that I am in the Father and the Father is in me? The words that I say to you I do not speak on my own; but the Father who dwells in me does his works. Believe me that I am in the Father and the Father is in me" (John 14:10-11). This language of communion between the Father and the Son reflects unity but also distinction. We see the same kind of language a few verses later when Jesus describes the indwelling advocate, the Holy Spirit, who comes from the Father and the Son: "he abides with [us], and he will be in [us]" (John

14:17). Our participation in this communion, Jesus says, comes as we love him. We show we love Jesus by doing what he commands (John 14:15)—the very way the Son shows love for the Father.

We find this same kind of language and desire expressed by Jesus in John 17. He longs for us to share in the very intimacy that the Son has with the Father. Here Jesus' prayer and hope is for all those who belong to him. He also indicates that there is a purposeful trajectory for our communion with God: "As you, Father, are in me and I am in you, may they also be in us, so that the world may believe that you have sent me. . . . I in them and you in me, that they may become completely one, so that the world may know that you have sent me and have loved them even as you have loved me" (John 17:21, 23).

The outcome of our dwelling in the communion of Father, Son and Spirit is that the reality of God's love will be evident to a love-starved world. Our worship will show love and justice. That is the very kind of worship for which we are being re-created.

For thirty years Kit Danley has been offering this sort of community in central Phoenix among a complex population, comprised predominantly of generationally poor Latinos, multitribal Native Americans, African Americans, poor whites and a few Asians. As founder and leader of Neighborhood Ministries, she has served and been loved and cared for by these people whose lives tell varied stories. *Raw, beautiful, dependent, vulnerable, unstable, gifted, loving, violent*—these are just some of the words that could describe the people she has sought to love. In what she calls the messiness of authentic community, God meets them in the worship of their daily lives and traumas as they discover the riches of true powerlessness, which is the cornerstone of humble worship. This is life in the heart of God's communion.

A transformative theme that has emerged for Kit and her Neighborhood Ministries is that worship and justice both depend on acknowledging true desperation. They must realize that they are empty-handed before (and with) those they seek to serve. As Kit says, it's when people face their inadequacies and their emptiness that they start to ask, "How desperate am I, for God or for justice?" That's when they begin to lay down the assumptions and prerogatives that hinder truly meeting and living for God. Jesus said we must lay down our lives to find them.

The Reordering of Reality

These are not mere words—theological poetry spun by Jesus and echoed by others. Instead it is the language that seeks to name what we will find to be "abundantly far more than all we can ask or imagine" (Ephesians 3:20). This is the context in which we are meant to live. Its unfamiliarity and apparent elusiveness is perhaps because we have heard it only from a distance or through the fog of our sleep.

To see and live that in Christ we are alive in God in the world is to reorder everyday reality. Faithful worship helps us claim this new life. If we live through Christ in the Father by the Spirit, we begin to see things right side up. Life in Christ is a step into reality. To live in the triune being of God through our adoption in Christ is to move into the deep and lasting mysteries of God's heart. It is to our great loss that all this can seem so foreign and unexplored. We can't even imagine the possibility of God's glorious reward, as C. S. Lewis writes: "Our Lord finds our desires not too strong but too weak. We are like half-hearted creatures who fool about with sex and drink and ambition when infinite joy is offered us. We are like children who would rather go on making mud-pies in a slum because we cannot imagine what is meant by the offer of a holiday at the sea. We are far too easily pleased."[2]

The Problems of Moving

Let's take stock of the challenge once again: the work of spiritual transformation, by which we come to live in God in the midst of our neighborhood, is the most difficult process in the universe. This is not an overstatement. After all, it required the death of the Son of God to accomplish it. To live in the reordered reality of life in God is to have an entirely different perspective about everything. Life is turned right side up, even though it will often feel like the opposite.

The radical force of this reorientation is captured in the closing scenes of the movie *The Truman Show,* when Truman faces just such a transformative process. Truman was born and raised on the sound stage of a television program that he believes is real life. In fact, though, he is the only real person within his artificial world. When cracks in his apparent reality appear, Truman literally sails away, taking a considerable risk to try to get away from the peculiar, constrained and inconsistent world around him. Just when Truman thinks he has made it through the fierce storm, the bow of his boat punctures the sky. What seems like an open vista turns out to be the painted shell of the sound stage.

Reality punctures Truman's universe, and everything changes. Truman could go back home, but he would never be the same, for his "home" is gone. At the poignant climax of the movie, Truman opens the door that will lead out into the real world. Before he steps across the threshold, the mastermind behind the TV show speaks to Truman from "the heavenlies." He wants Truman to stay in his world, offering him a better life than he will find outside the bubble of the sound stage. Truman asks him, "Who are you?" The producer, whose name is Christof, says, "I am the creator." Truman asks, "And who am I?" "You," he says, "you are the star!" Truman faces the illusions that speak to him, the appearance of reality. What he chooses as he steps through the door is the true reality. This marks the reordering of everything, and the recasting and refocusing of his life will become the rest of his story.

Reality punctures the universe and everything changes. This is the work of the gospel. It's called being born again, waking up and responding to the reality of God's love in Christ. It's finding our life in the One in whom "all things hold together" (Colossians 1:17). No wonder this can be disorienting. No wonder we find it hard to grasp and difficult to live out. Stepping through the door is not easy because it requires moving from the familiar to the unfamiliar. But it is the only way to true life. It is not that everything else is unreal, but we must face the illusions. Our families, bodies, houses, jobs, relationships and work are real, but we come to see our lives and our reality differently, recast in the context of God's triune life.

Every time we pray we speak what is now our first language of love in Christ. We can cultivate this in many ways in order to speak fluently and listen wisely. I try to do this by living each day as an act of prayer. All of my activities, whether driving along the road, walking through the neighborhood, running errands, going to soccer games, grocery shopping, making plans, talking on the phone, exercising or eating dinner with my family can become an exercise in claiming the love of God. I like to look carefully at the people I see throughout the day and consciously claim God's love for them.

When possible, I try to go out of my way to engage the needs I could just as easily ignore. I have made it an annual practice to choose one part of the world and read everything I can about that area and its needs over the course of the year. I have found that giving toward the needs of others, whether those nearby or far off, is easier with a visible reminder, like a giving jar on the kitchen table. As a frequent book buyer, I discipline my spending (and my reading) by setting aside the same amount I spend for myself to give toward buying books for the church in the developing world. I've traveled to places of need, praying that God would sear the realities of the people there into my heart so that I do not forget. These are small ways of growing in God's love for those I may not otherwise think about, let alone truly love.

Both the profound and the mundane are changed when we live in our true home. When we step into our new address in God, we find we have deeper resources to face our problems. Take family issues as an example.

However good, bad or indifferent our parents, they are just human. They are not God, but like us they are created and loved by God and are often lost and confused in their relationship to God. Whether in their sacrifices or fits of immaturity, in their hard work or self-absorbed distractions, in their desire to be wise or in their mixed messages, parents' strengths and weaknesses reflect an imperfect reality and make it clear that we need another home, a better one.

Or take our work. We face our tasks in homes, schools, offices, job sites, hospitals, courts or elsewhere. We may like our day's work, or we may not. Often it absorbs the most and the best of our time. The reordering work of life in Christ in God changes each day's labor by placing it in the context of God's vision so that we work in the sight and the presence of God whatever our work is. It's easy to go off to work and assume God is somewhere else. But it's a lie and a loss to do so. God is there on the job site, in on the phone call, the commute, the Internet and with our irritating colleague or boss. This reorders our view so we see what is in fact already true about our life. And it changes everything to live this out: we now dwell in God in our workplace.

Laurie, a social worker, fights every day for at-risk children. Her caseload and the layers of bureaucracy she faces each day make her work extremely enervating. She often feels overwhelmed because she knows it could be so different, but inevitably it is not. Laurie easily gets drawn into the deep suffering and injustice that certain children live with. In the face of those challenges, in finding the ability to endure with love, she silently claims God's tender love for her and for each child and family in crisis. Laurie's work is changed as she holds each child in her heart, knowing that their lives and hers are in God's heart.

Looking at our world from the window of God's heart means we don't see need in the same way. Words like "I would never be that stupid" to live in Pakistan, for example, may still be in our hearts, but such words clearly are not in God's heart. As we grow in our faith and our knowledge of God, we internalize that "it was while we were yet stupid" that Christ died for us. We begin to realize we live in the heart of One who sought us in our need and poured out his life for our sake and who now wants us to do the same for others. Worship that is done "in spirit and in truth" reveals how far we have to go, but it doesn't let us off the hook. Worship gradually realigns our hearts, our actions and our priorities with God's. We learn that we now live in a heart big enough to hold all suffering in hope and in justice.

The Strange New World

The triune God welcomes us home into the loving, serving communion that is God's life. We dwell there as we go about our jobs, raise children, worry about money, grieve, go to school, plan for retirement, have sex, attend church, help with homework, vote, watch TV, laugh, pray and do thousands of other ordinary things. Living in this new environment gives us a new taste of the meaning of relationship: it is not self-serving, not just about getting our needs met, not about winning. These lessons are the life's work of serious disciples, although it would be foolish to expect to completely master them.

When we live in God in the world, we see everything, whether on the other side of the world or down the street, in a new way. The primary lens is no longer our family background, our personality, prejudices, worries or subculture; it is now the love of God for every person. Only when I practice living in God do I realize that I am secure enough to not be self-absorbed, I am free enough to not exploit it. I am gifted and called to express the passions of God's heart for the poor and the needy, the oppressed and the suffering. In doing this, you often find that God is so deeply present with such people that the blessing you receive is greater than the sacrifice you offer. While this is not the primary point, it is part of God's unexpected benediction.

6   Doing Justice Starts with Rest

A LIFE THAT WORSHIPS AND DOES JUSTICE STARTS WITH REST.
Scripture's call to seek justice surely involves action, considerable and
costly. But a life that does justice rises out of worship, which starts with
rest, is sustained by rest and returns to rest. This may seem counter-
intuitive, but let's reconsider it.

Rest

Genesis tells us that after six days of creating, God rested. So God is not
obsessive-compulsive (surely some of the plants could have stood some
trimming!), nor is he manic. God is not desperate, not worried, not a
handwringer. God gives creation extraordinary freedom, which is soon
squandered, and still God rests. Nowhere is there a suggestion that God
had second thoughts about that day off—*If only I hadn't rested, maybe
Adam and Eve . . .*

In fact, God later called Israel to mirror this priority. The Lord commanded them to rest (Deuteronomy 5:12-15). Every seven days they
were to rest. God's call for Israel to practice sabbath living was given so
they would never be more than six days away from laying down the im-
plements and practices of their own productivity in order to acknowledge that human life was set within a limited boundary of time, place
and responsibility. This sabbath practice was meant to be an exercise in
human freedom and liberty.

Acknowledging these boundaries sets us free to be human. The message is this: prepare for the sabbath; go to sleep and wake up knowing that your life and the world do not belong to you or depend on you; worship God, and remember with his people the One who made you and the world, and called you his own; don't work; don't rely on your provision; then live this out today and every other day of the week, including doing justice.

We may live this side of the cross and resurrection of Christ, but if we are to live life in the context God intends, we also need to live in this sabbath reality. We are to live it daily as well as practice a weekly sabbath-keeping. It is not just an old legalism reinserting itself. It says to the frantic, exhausted, distracted, fatigued people of God: please, rest. The hectic lives of Christians in our culture and the busyness of many churches show little sign of living out of God's rest. Our tendencies to imitate our culture are directly related to our unwillingness to stop, cease producing, consuming, moving, accomplishing, buying, planning. We can be as much 24-7 (even in the name of Jesus) as our secular neighbors. Yet we cannot live as light and salt, doing righteousness and showing justice, if we fail to practice living out of God's rest. It's a boundary that sets us free.

In the story of Shadrach, Meshach and Abednego, we see that Nebuchadnezzar used mesmerizing rhythms and sounds to get people to bow before his idol: "when you hear the sound of the horn, pipe, lyre, . . . you are to fall down and worship the golden statue that King Nebuchadnezzar has set up" (Daniel 3:5). Shadrach, Meshach and Abednego are different because they are not lulled by that rhythm. They have practiced remembering who they are. They have stopped regularly to show for themselves and for the sake of others that their lives are not their own, and neither are they Nebuchadnezzar's. They belong to God alone, however dire their environment.

Jim is a twentysomething man in our congregation. While growing up, he watched his father succeed in business, but Jim did not want to approach his life in the same way. Jim never knew anybody who worked harder than his dad, but neither did Jim find true satisfaction in his father's example. Instead Jim wanted to bring his faith to every aspect of his life, including his busy job. He was impressed by the faithfulness of Muslim colleagues, and their devotion to their own religious practices challenged Jim in his. Soon after 9/11, Jim resolved to adopt a pattern of deliberate praying for five to ten minutes, five times a day. Recently he told me that though he had tried every technogadget available, none of them had helped him order his life like the practice of simply ceasing to work and stopping to pray, worshiping midstream in his daily life. His priorities and habits have changed. Jim said, "I still want to succeed, but the measure I am using is constantly refined by this discipline."

Our church staff and lay leaders periodically do an inventory of what is essential in our work and ministries. Recently we have considered how our leadership has wrongly contributed to a busyness that actually undermines the deeper work of the Holy Spirit. We realize that sometimes we have inadvertently contributed to a fatigue that is not necessarily honoring to God, even though it is well-intentioned. Because I have great stamina, I can be the worst judge of when enough is enough—or way too much! I need the help of the body of Christ to know when to stop. It is hard to say no to ourselves and to our latest and greatest ideas. But those are the moments we need to consider again what it means to let go and live out of God's rest.

The Gift of Release

Sabbath-keeping—living in ways that say yes to God and his rhythms and no to the life-draining rhythms of the culture and people around us—is essential to our call to worship that does justice. Our response to injustice in the world is to be evident daily. Our capacity to know and understand injustice is clarified by being with the God who is just, whose nature is violated by every injustice, who suffers with every injustice in the world. Injustice, then, is first and foremost defined by God, not by humans.

By sabbath-keeping we lay down our definitions and perspectives of injustice, our activities for the cause of justice, our power and assumptions, and we then have the chance to hear from God. The Lord is the central target of his creatures' abuse of power, yet he alone holds both the full scope of the problem and offers the true hope for its resolution. We are mere ambassadors. We seek and worship the God who is the answer to injustice. The sabbath-keeping practice of worship helps us stop long enough to remember these baselines and have our reality recast at the start of each week.

Allison was one of the interns who came to Phoenix to serve alongside Kit Danley at the Neighborhood Ministries. She came from an upper-middle-class background; her father was Anglo and her mother Mexican American. Allison, whose gifts and talents are many, was raised to step toward an even more power-filled life, with every opportunity for success in her education and career. Only when she stepped into the needy Mexican subculture in Phoenix did she begin the most important transformation of her life. Her life had been marked by patterns of hiddenness—she would hardly have acknowledged her own Mexican heritage; she had not realized how much her capacities to perform and produce masked her insecurities and drove her to make her life, including her spiritual life, a product of her control and achievement. For Allison, God's rest has been an invitation to face some of her greatest fears and to lay down some of the dysfunctional ways she has tried to avoid or cope with them. In that journey, she has found her life.

No doubt, our direct knowledge and awareness of injustice in the world is a profound and provocative part of our call to do justice. But that is not the deepest and most sustained part of our call. All of the reasons for this are made clearer by the rest that is God's and is meant to be ours. First the church needs to remember that justice is God's business.

God's people are important but are secondary players in this cause. The gospel underlines that only God can establish peace and justice. Faithful worship shows that God is relentless in this and wants to use us in the effort. But God calls us to live out of his rest, which teaches us in matters of injustice, as in all else, that we do not have the final authority or responsibility.

Friends of mine who serve on the frontlines of the battle for justice admit they have a hard time remembering this or at least practicing it. This is understandable given the vortex of human need that is nonstop, overwhelming, without end or rest. Jesus himself faced this pressure. When a woman breaks an alabaster jar of perfume to pour on Jesus, those watching are scandalized because it could have been sold and the money given to the poor (Mark 14:3-5). Jesus gives an unexpected answer: "You always have the poor with you. . . . She has done what she could" (Mark 14:7-8). There is always the possibility of doing something more, something better. But in God's rest, there is room for a simple offering, lovingly and earnestly made, even if others might call it a waste.

Practicing biblical rest in some pattern of sabbath-keeping is not a sign of abdication, nor arrogance, nor bourgeois indulgence. Instead it means we stop at least once a week to remember that we are not God. Whatever our passion for justice, whatever our success or failure in seeking justice, we need to remember that even when we are most sure we are doing God's business, we are not God. Justice is God's business. We are simply invited to have a stake in what is God's, and God's alone, to bring about.

The history of Christian social justice movements is littered with examples of people who failed to practice this. To many activists, spiritual rest does not seem like it is doing anything. But that's the point. It's not doing anything except remembering and practicing what's most important: trusting God to be God over all. If we are just waking up to God and his passion for justice, we might think the first thing to do is get as busy as we possibly can. After all, *there's injustice in the world, and God wants us to do something about it!* This can quickly become the headline screaming at us each day. We might start reading Worldwatch reports, poring over Amnesty International descriptions of suffering and injustice, watching CNN's international coverage, and reading every Sojourners e-mail. We might attend meetings and community action groups several nights a week, working in soup kitchens, assisting in letter campaigns and giving financial support to the needs we see—and still feel like we aren't doing anything, at least not compared to the scope of the need. In some ways that's true!

In such moments we may start down the road to burnout, which can kill what God is fanning to life. Or we may become bitter and judgmental toward the inertness of others around us. We find ourselves on an airplane or on the commuter bus or with our church family in Sunday worship wanting to stand up and scream, "What are *you* doing about suffering and injustice?" Even a modest degree of awareness of the global scale of injustice can overwhelm us. Clearly, we are inadequate. All of us together are inadequate. Or we may give in to a third temptation, which is to surrender to inaction because this enterprise, even life itself, seems all for naught. This is when we need to remember the larger perspective that can save us. As Mother Teresa put it, "We ourselves feel that what we are doing is just a drop in the ocean, but the ocean would be less because of that missing drop."[1]

I have made trips to the developing world to learn about the needy and the poor and have found myself overwhelmed by the breadth of the problems. The last time I returned from Africa, this sense of discouragement was even greater than usual. Although I saw some wonderful examples of God's light and mercy in ordinary and extraordinary ways, the sum of what is happening in Africa (and other places) is still overwhelming. The many and intractable patterns of suffering seem to remove any hope of true light.

I am learning to let the discouragement itself be a call to identify with the suffering. It is also a call to the deeper spiritual labor of seeking and claiming God's hope and acting on what can be done. The issue is not our pain in trying to figure out how to cope with such a world. The point is to be God's people of genuine hope to the world. It's not our pain as an outsider that matters, but the reality of those who have little outside their pain. To step into such need instead of running away, we need to live in God's rest.

Daniel is a ten-year-old boy I met outside Kitgum, Uganda. He was one of several hundred other children who had come in the dark to this "night commuter" camp for two reasons: to sleep and to avoid for one more night being kidnapped by a marauding band of the Lord's Resistance Army. This tyrannous "army" was established by Joseph Kony nearly twenty years ago as a kind of political resistance movement. Kony's rhetoric sought to establish a Uganda founded on his own version of the Ten Commandments, but his tactics have been perverse to the extreme. His army is largely composed of children, ages five to eighteen, who are conscripted into his psychopathic service. They are kidnapped, tortured and enslaved in Kony's random acts of violence all over northern Uganda. During these past two decades, approximately 1.8 million people have become displaced by fear of his brutality.

The night I met Daniel, he and the other children would find spots in an open schoolroom, without screens or mosquito netting, and sleep on hard mats on the cement floor—again. Like many others, Daniel does this every night, as he has since the age of five. We sang some Christian choruses before offering a bedtime prayer: "Lord be with all the children tonight. Keep them safe from being kidnapped. Keep them free from disease and worry. Be with their parents in their displacement camps, and keep them safe too. Thank you that you are here tonight, right here in the darkness, fear and uncertainty. Thank you that you love us and will be with us."

As we prayed, Daniel's face was earnest. He raised a small handmade cross over his head and whispered yes to each petition. As I talked to Daniel afterward, he explained that the cross was made from the *chwa* tree, whose dense, strong wood made it an ideal instrument of punishment or abuse whenever one of Kony's young soldiers "deserved" it. For former abductees, making these crosses from the same wood becomes an act of spiritual reimagination: God takes the very worst, enters into it and is crucified for the hope of the world. In the place of suffering, God offers life instead of death. God's rest was Daniel's only hope and comfort. Daniel is so right to say yes.

The Renewing Water of Worship

Predictably, when our communal and personal sabbath-keeping practices are anemic or absent, we have far less to give for the sake of others. Sunday morning worship is seen as discretionary to soccer games and long breakfasts. Personal Bible study is reduced to a kind of spiritual slot machine, where we hope for a jackpot to help us along the way, instead of being an experience that leads us into an entirely different frame of life. We underestimate the daily and weekly discipline of worship that is required to recalibrate the context that shapes our lives.

What we need is a liberated sabbath-keeping practice. This means that daily, certainly weekly, we are to unhook from both the subtle and blatant ways we let the rhythms of life and culture, instead of God, tell us who we are and how we are to live. The goal is to find liberation from the lies or half-truths of our culture and the freedom to give and receive love, mercy and justice. Sabbath-keeping has to be a key part of this liberation.

If we don't lift our heads to see God in worship, we can't see what God wants to show us, which includes our neighbor. Then our neighbor becomes those we choose to see, not those God wants us to see. Worship draws us into the heart of God, and as we live there, we see the neighbors

God gives us: the forgotten, the marginalized, the poor, the oppressed. We may have chosen to live in a certain enclave for the specific reason of avoiding such neighbors. If our sabbath-keeping practices put "going to church" on the same list as shopping, surfing the Internet, eating, working or any other hands-on-the-controls-of-life activity, then we will never see those other neighbors. And certainly we will not see them through the heart of God.

If on the other hand our sabbath-keeping practices awaken us to God, cause us to confess our self-absorbed lives, draw us into a deepening Christian life and move us back into the other six days of the week with a fresh vision and a reminder of who we are, who our neighbors are and where we live, then things begin to change. "But—a seventh of our time!" some might object. "No, all of your time," Jesus could rightly respond. "Only a seventh, at least a seventh, to keep you on track with all the rest of the time I am entrusting to you."

Our engagement in works of justice arises out of a worshipful life. It comes not out of being activists but out of living in God's rest, every day. This is one of the most profound aspects of a Christian social ethic. It is not that we are meant to find our lives by being community organizers. It is that, as we live in the rest of God, we live in our true home, in the heart of God in Christ, in whom "all things hold together. . . . Through him God was pleased to reconcile to himself all things, whether on earth or in heaven, by making peace through the blood of his cross" (Colossians 1:17, 20).

We engage not out of desperation but out of hope, not superficially but sacrificially. We enter not as those who are standing in for a god who is absent, but to make evident the God who is already there and who holds us in his heart. We are the broken who are being healed, and we are the brothers and sisters of those who share our need. Like us, they hunger for the good news of God's redemptive love. This is found in lives and practices of worship that nourish, motivate and sustain.

This is the ordinary life that is intended for Christ's followers. But Ron Sider's book *The Scandal of the Evangelical Conscience* painfully details just how untrue it is for many gospel-seeking, gospel-trusting people in America. It seems our consciences have been bought by the surrounding cultural forces that define *ordinary* in very different terms. So we now consider it ordinary that people spend countless hours before electronic gadgets that largely isolate us from face-to-face social interaction: games, videos, computers, television. Yet we follow a Lord who stopped a crowd to honor a rejected woman. We consider it ordinary that people don't have time for family or friends. Yet we follow a Lord who says we will be known by our love. We consider it ordinary that the almighty dollar gets the last word. Yet we follow a Lord who clothes the lilies of the field in more glory than Solomon's riches. We consider it ordinary that 1.5 million to 2.7 million die from malaria each year.[2] Yet we follow a Lord who offers us the bread of life. We think it is ordinary that more than a million children are forced into sex trafficking each year.[3] Yet we follow a Lord who says, "Let the little children come to me, and do not stop them; for it is to such as these that the kingdom of heaven belongs" (Matthew 19:14).

The gospel seeks to deliver us from this ordinary context. Worship gives us the chance to practice embodying God's rest, recasting how we see and respond to God and the world around us. If our worship does this, we can be the arms and legs of God by helping in the deliverance of others. If, however, we miss the life-shaping gift of saying no and yes based on sabbath-keeping rhythms rather than cultural rhythms, we easily forget what matters to the heart of God. If we can't say no to our desires for our own sake, how can we ever do it for the sake of those who suffer? If we don't dwell in the sacred heart of Jesus, then we have only our own hearts to motivate us to respond to the needs of the forgotten. While the human heart may take some people a long way, it doesn't take most of us very far at all. We need God's rest.

Sabbath Practices: Saying No and Saying Yes

Many other books have been written on sabbath-keeping, and I encourage you to pursue those helpful resources as well as to use your own imagination, in community with others, to develop life-giving sabbath practices. Here I will simply discuss two closely related directions in sabbath-keeping.

One movement in sabbath practices is saying no—to our agendas, schedules, to our production drive, our sense of time and urgency, to the busyness and patterns of every day, to our power, to our cultivated blindness. We never like saying no to ourselves. That's part of the gift and challenge of sabbath-keeping. This self-denial can make the whole exercise seem negative and legalistic. Living in a culture where so many people take their laptops and cell phones on vacation only reinforces how far we are from grasping the meaning of rest. But legalistic self-denial is not the spirit in which God gives us the sabbath. Instead it's about stepping away from the ordinary in order to be restored.

Pastors, worship leaders and lay leaders often face a particular challenge in sabbath-keeping. When Sunday is the busiest and most demanding day of the week, it is hard to experience it as a source of rest. For such people, this may mean that sabbath-keeping has to occur some other way. Perhaps another day can be found during the week, apart from the "day off" for chores and errands. It should be a day of doing nothing but the most essential activities.

Even this may not always be possible. In my own experience, a busy Sunday can be marked by God's rest if I am internally prepared to enter it that way. If I go into a Sunday focused on my performance or just distracted in some way, I seldom find the gift of rest. But if I enter the day prepared for rest, I have found it possible to lead worship, and worship at the same time, as well as to find deep quiet.

Another practice has recently helped me claim the sabbath even on Sundays. The pastors on our staff now meet earlier than we used to so we can have a longer and more relaxed time of prayer with one another. Our love and affection for each other as well as our partnership in the gospel and in the day before us means that just sitting together in God's presence is quieting and renewing. We long to enter together into God's rest, and we share a mutual desire that each of us and each member of our congregation does so too.

This first movement in sabbath-keeping is about getting unhooked from the mesmerizing rhythms that set the patterns of daily life. We say no to those, and it's like being granted permission to live out of an entirely different mode than the one handed to us by our production-driven, multitasking, consumer-oriented culture. This mode is called God's rest. We desperately need it, particularly if we want to seek justice.

Sabbath practices are also invaluable in daily life. They quiet us and refocus us. They help us enact our dependence upon the true God and keep the voices of surrounding idols at bay. Whether on our own or with family or colleagues, we can make sabbath rest part of our daily routine with simple acts: saying no to phone calls or e-mail for thirty minutes or an hour each day, or reducing the time we normally spend watching television. Having a friend share in the same practice at the same time each day can be a great help.

The other movement in sabbath practices is saying yes to God and yes to the world God has given us. Here energy is focused toward re-creation and seeking the renewal of mind and body that comes from seeking and resting in God. Just as there are many things to say no to, so there are many different ways to say yes to God. But the idea is not to set aside a day for myself, asking, "What do I want to do today?" That would make it even more self-focused than the average day! Although we may need a day like that occasionally, it is not a sabbath. In sabbath-keeping, we seek God and the things of God. We are quiet ourselves in order to listen, love, worship, ponder, offer, sacrifice and recast what we are doing in our life.

We say yes to God by affirming and seeking to be in his presence and by hearing and living in response to his Word. We say yes to God's people by seeking to face one another, to lean into deeper friendship, to create extended time to just be together without hurry for an afternoon or evening, to eat, talk, listen, care, laugh, seek or encourage. It is not a time to repay social obligations but to be with and to build up the body of Christ. It's more about being than doing.

Think about creating your own sabbath practices. How might you spend unstructured time with friends? What would enliven your imagination in the things of God? What might you do outdoors to be reminded of the beauty of God's creation? When could you schedule an uninterrupted conversation with someone you really care about? If you have children, could you spend time with them away from their "stuff," playing a game together inside or outside? How might you practice offering a "sacrifice of thanksgiving" to God each week as a family? What simple thing could you do on a sabbath that you ordinarily have no time for but that would really be nurturing to your soul? How might you spend part of the day meditating and considering the forgotten, the needy or the poor? How might you claim God's rest and God's justice and mercy for them?

One of my own sabbath routines has been to pray for the world in different ways. Sometimes I give extended attention to a particular country of need. Other times I pray for individuals I know who live in different parts of the world. Some families with young children have told me that letting a child point to a spot on a globe can be a great tool for engaging in prayer. We can use the Internet to see images from the other side of the world, which can be a great help in making other people's lives and needs more visible and tangible to us. Another visual resource to help stimulate our thoughts of others' lives is the book *Material World: A Global Family Portrait* by Peter Menzel or *Hope in the Dark* by Jena Lee and Jeremy Cowart. All of these activities can be sabbath rest.

The practice of sabbath-keeping might be a big lifestyle change for many people. It is like the challenge facing a person who is just beginning to tithe; he has not yet learned that the way to be content with what he has is to give more of it away. Likewise, for those who feel like there is never enough time, it is hard to imagine that the best way to find enough time is to set more of it aside for God's rest. That is actually the rhythm that nourishes and focuses our lives and discipleship in the way God intends. Then there will be time to do justice.

The sabbath practices of saying no and saying yes both have the goal of unhooking from culture and daily routines and reconnecting with the heart and mind of God and his purposes in the world. They are meant to be life-affirming for the purposes and plans of God, for the things that will help us remember our humanity, and for reclaiming God's reordering of our reality in terms that express God's role and identity. This is the restoration that gives us the will and the heart to live a life worthy of the gospel—a life that is awake to God and the world.

7 | When Worship Talks to Power

WHEN WE AVOID THE REAL DANGERS OF WORSHIP, we miss one of its primary gifts: the realignment of power. Safe worship stymies this essential reconstructive work. Yet it is central to the kingdom of God and its vision of justice. The realignment of power is fundamental to the cause of justice because much of the twisted soul of injustice is the abuse of power. Whether the injustice is poverty, bonded slavery, land grabbing, forced prostitution, hunger, rape or racism, we find the abuse of power. Likewise, an abuse of power is at play even in more mundane examples of injustice: gossip, manipulation, coercion, lying, deception or libel. At the core of it all lies an abuse of power. Nothing thwarts God's purposes more than twisted power; nothing renews God's purposes more than redeeming power.

There are many reasons that worship and justice are inextricable, but the central one is the reality that Jesus is Lord (Romans 10:9; 1 Corinthians 12:3). Worship acknowledges and bows, explores and confesses, seeks and depends upon God's power. Justice searches and reflects, weighs and suffers, identifies and demonstrates God's power in all relationships.

When we look at it this way, Christian worship—corporate and individual—can and should be one of the most profound and relevant responses to power abuse in the world. In worship we cast our lives upon the faithful and just power of God. When we do so, we oppose all acts of unjust power. The gospel of Jesus Christ is about God's remarkable initiative and grace marshaled to realign power: the power of sin, evil, suffering, injustice and death. God confronts and seeks to challenge various forms of power abuse, whether in relation to himself (Adam and Eve's assertion of their will over God's) or in relation to one another (Adam and Eve, Jacob and Esau, Abraham and Sarah, or Joseph and his brothers). The first and second commandments are a positive affirmation of God's true and just power alignment. In the gospel, the matchless and invincible heart of God confronts and defeats the heart of darkness and death. In its unexpected, power-inverting way, the sacrificial love of God in "Christ crucified" (1 Corinthians 1:23-24) recasts all forms of power. That's the work and meaning of the cross. Our worship helps us remember this power realignment so we can live differently because of it.

In 1994 Gary Haugen was assigned by the Department of Justice to lead the United Nation's investigation into the Rwandan genocide. Every day he counted thousands more dead bodies. Every day he looked into the heart of human evil at point-blank range. Returning home to his wonderful wife and family from this horrific responsibility was reverse culture shock, to put it mildly. Clearly, life was going to be different.

I know Gary well and have often asked him why he isn't still paralyzed by the trauma of his time in Rwanda. I have a feeling I might be if I had gone through what he did. Gary's response is usually something like, "That wouldn't be helpful." So much is embedded in that simple response. When Gary came back from Rwanda, he joined with others to found the International Justice Mission (IJM), and he now serves as its president. This organization does the dangerous and much-needed work of delivering people from their oppressors and bringing the perpetrators to justice. This is not just a reflection of Gary's good mental health or his ability to take constructive steps forward, though both are true. In founding IJM, Gary demonstrates that by God's grace, he is more caught up in responding to the suffering of others than in his own response. What delivers him from himself and has allowed him to establish and lead the remarkable human-rights ministry that IJM has become is Gary's deep confidence that Jesus Christ is Lord. That reality, which he has come to know through worship with God's people, in middle-class America and in places of suffering around the world, has taught him that the God he worships holds authority over every power and principality, even though he has seen some of the most vivid expressions of evil in the world. The IJM staff has a daily chapel time, a sabbath rest to say to God and to remind themselves that what they do is only possible by God's power, not their own. Gary and the others at IJM know that the gospel realigns power, and they remember that in their worship.

The recalibrating of power, which was done at the cross and is remembered in our practices of worship, will transform our lives. Worship helps us go back to work or school on Monday with a revised picture of whose power really matters. We hear the morning news about how cuts in government or job layoffs affect the poor, and our worship informs and changes our response to those facts. Worship also changes how we see our own personal power and helps us remember to show our power in love toward all those we meet, whether family, friend, neighbor or foe.

Worship helps us remember that the greatest power we could ever hope to have is the power of self-offering love, especially toward those who may see us as enemies. Worship also reminds us that there is now a power at work in us that is greater than any form of power we may encounter in the world. Further, that power is not for our sake only, but for the sake of our living out of that power to enact justice and mercy in the world.

A Power Problem

Our practices of worship seldom take these issues of power so seriously, however. Middle-class American churches typically identify with the culture, so there is little desire or demand to question power. Since the systems of our culture work for us (especially in the white, educated middle class), we readily believe in the general benevolence of government or education or commerce or welfare or justice. This inoculates us against facing and engaging issues of power abuse in the world.

I am still stunned when I hear statistics like these: that more than 25 million people around the world today live in slavery;[1] that 40 percent of the world's population lacks basic sanitation facilities and over one billion use unsafe water;[2] that in the least developed countries over 50 percent of the population is not expected to live to the age of sixty, compared to just over 10 percent in the most developed countries;[3] that the per capita spending on police in India is about twenty-five cents per person per year, whereas in the United States it is over $250 per person per year.[4] And India is better off than countries where no police force even exists, such as Liberia and Chad. In other countries the local police would be the last place to go for help in the face of injustice, because of graft and corruption. We assume that the basic protection of law enforcement most in the United States enjoy is more or less present in other parts of the world, but it's not. Many people in other countries, especially the poor, are exposed to whims of power abuse, and the police are but one example.

Corporate and individual worship should lay out the power cards of life before the One who alone holds all power. The gospel redefines each card. Some cards we leave on the altar: pride, manipulation, lying, deception and coercion. Some cards we pick up again and in humility offer them to the world: health, education, race, opportunity, responsibility, friendship, advocacy or sacrifice. Or, on the most basic level, having enough to eat, a bed to sleep in, a home to live in, a school or a job.

Instead, the churches that get the most attention, and thereby influence what is thought to matter in church life, are those with the most power. Megachurches offer an extreme example. Like the values of our culture, it seems the bigger and more alluring the church, the better. They are a study in power. On a positive note, such churches have passed along many benefits to smaller churches, often in the form of conferences and other resources. But the power of megachurches is not neutral. Their influence mounts through their capitalization of forms of power that mirror the culture: size, money, fame, influence, expertise, drivenness, show. These are forms of power our culture is already addicted to. Yet megachurches never seem to undergo any transparent self-criticism about their own power. It would be significant if one of the megachurches of our nation chose by grace to find ways of divesting itself of or at least redistributing power.

I know of just such a bold experiment happening in a church in Nairobi, Kenya. Nairobi Chapel had grown into a megachurch, with thousands of people from all over Nairobi coming to worship weekly. The pastor and church leaders began to realize that they had too much power concentrated in their middle-class church in comparison to Kibera, a slum that is home to one million people in their city. Surely, they reasoned, God has given us the power to share the gospel among the poor as well as (or more than) the middle class.

After careful reflection and wise discernment, the leaders decided to close Nairobi Chapel. They subdivided the church into five smaller congregations, seeking to establish churches that would combine the poorest with the middle class. Their decision to redistribute their institutional power can only be explained by kingdom values.

Our worship is meant to be the catalyst for the primary work of God's kingdom. But rather than stimulating such transformed lives, our current worship practices emasculate its true potency. The atmosphere of most churches seems to communicate that power is benign, whether in reference to the power of certain people, relationships, institutions or governments. Even if churches address issues of personal power for the cause of piety or perseverance, they usually do not address the injustices of the more pervasive cultural or institutional power. Most of us in American churches don't hear mention of gangs or school closings or corner-store muggings or welfare cuts. We don't hear about the homeless or health-care inequalities. This silence fits the landscape of much middle-class culture. So we don't see that our worship needs to call any of this into question—until we allow the gospel and our worship to speak to the problem of power abuse.

The Power of Liturgy

Many of the classical elements of Christian worship are invaluable tools for confronting power abuse. It would be a great help if we let these elements speak to us. The best liturgies of Christian worship, whether high-church or low-church, mainline or evangelical, offer protocols for understanding power, unmasking its illusions and realigning our limits as well as our vocations in relation to power. The root of the word *liturgy* means "the work of the people." As we do this work in grace, it becomes part of our transformation.

In speaking of classic liturgical elements, I do not intend to affirm any particular tradition or style of worship, nor do I want to imply that liturgical forms are a spiritual delivery system. In fact, these liturgical practices can just be categories of daily living. What I am attempting to do is to see these elements theologically and historically as windows into important aspects of worship that take different liturgical forms. Whatever those may be, the church has long had the theological tools it needs. How we express them can be found as appropriately in an emergent service as in a high-church service.

Worship can teach us about true power, lead us to recognize and redefine false power, and commission us in the kind of gospel power that equips us for our mission of seeking justice, loving mercy and walking humbly before God. Let's look at what each liturgical element can teach us about power.

Call to Worship

We do not call ourselves to worship; God calls us. Throughout Scripture, the call to worship is given only by God and reframes everything else in the worship service that follows it as well as in life. "Hear, O Israel: The LORD is our God, the LORD alone. You shall love the LORD your God with all your heart, and with all your soul, and with all your might" (Deuteronomy 6:4-5).

If we understand what it truly is, we see the call to worship as an invitation beyond all other power. In the midst of the world's cacophony of disordered powers, God calls us to bow before the power that is above all others. This word of unexcelled power and unparalleled authority comes both as command and invitation. Unlike ours, God's power never overreaches. God's power is without manipulation. God's call to worship is not like any other call by powerful people in our lives: our boss, friends, parents, spouse, teacher or our culture. The call to worship is not indirect or mediated power, but God gives it to all who have ears: "Come to me, all you that are weary and are carrying heavy burdens, and I will give you rest. Take my yoke upon you, and learn from me; for I am gentle and humble in heart, and you will find rest for your souls. For my yoke is easy, and my burden is light" (Matthew 11:28-30).

At the very start of worship, the Lord invites all who have ears to hear. This call goes to God's people as a whole as well as to individuals. The qualification we bring is our neediness, not our stature. We may have come to worship homeless or having many worldly possessions, but the only way anyone comes is by invitation. God calls us all to worship. No one person has greater privilege than anyone else. In God's presence, no donor chart places someone higher up or closer in. The call is based on the power and grace of God, not on our own power or worthiness. It places everyone on even ground. God is not intimidated or impressed by human power. God, in the power of love and communion, freedom and grace, invites us to "approach the throne of grace with boldness" (Hebrews 4:16).

Prayer of Adoration

God deserves adoration, however and whenever it is acknowledged in the worship service. We offer what should be given to no one and nothing else. Thanks, praise, gratitude—all these can be given to others as well as to God. But adoration is deserved by God alone. Adoration is an element of our sabbath rest, when we acknowledge that we bow in humility, praise and awe before the unmatched power of the living God.

Many of us and many in our world suffer daily from ordinary and extraordinary expressions of power abuse. We come to worship needing to name and find the power for life. I think of the couple struggling with infertility who sat in the front pew crying quietly this past Sunday. I think of the couple three rows behind them who temporarily separated because of his alcoholism as they seek the help that will restore their family. I think of the ways I am so inadequate as a pastor to be able to love or to lead as I think I should. I think of Elisabeth, the young girl I mentioned earlier, who was enslaved in a brothel in Asia.

When we adore God, we are turning to the true power that longs to give abundant life. Jesus Christ is "the way, and the truth, and the life" (John 14:6)—for the couple with infertility, for the family with addiction issues, for the inadequate pastor, and for the systems of lies and power abuse that held Elisabeth.

Our prayer of adoration is a declaration against all aberrant and destructive uses of power. It can also be an assault on our own self-adoration. It is also a reproach against any government, culture or individual that oppresses others. Adoration is deserved by only One; he is the rock of our salvation, the only One who is our peace.

Prayer of Confession

We only have the power to confess because we worship a God with the power to forgive. Like the father who ran to meet the prodigal and still loved the older brother, we are reminded that we can and must tell the truth about our need.

At one of the lowest moments of Israel's life, when Jerusalem had been besieged and the temple desecrated, Nehemiah sends for someone to bring him word about what has happened. Hearing the news of Jerusalem's devastation, Nehemiah pauses to grieve and to confess, or to tell the truth:

> When I heard these words I sat down and wept, and mourned for days, fasting and praying before the God of heaven. I said, "O LORD God of heaven, the great and awesome God who keeps covenant and steadfast love with those who love him and keep his commandments; let your ear be attentive and your eyes open to hear the prayer of your servant that I now pray before you day and night for your servants, the people of Israel, confessing the sins of the people of Israel, which we have sinned against you. Both I and my family have sinned. We have offended you deeply, failing to keep the commandments, the statutes, and the ordinances that you commanded your servant Moses. (Nehemiah 1:4-7)

Laments like Nehemiah's are common in the Old Testament. It underscores the need to name our failure to God before we can advance in hope. To find real hope often requires passing through the fire of confession.

When we confess, we take responsibility for our false or destructive uses of power. We admit and acknowledge our accountability. The prayer of confession takes us into the darkness of our own hearts and of the world. It declares the power of evil in and around us. It dares to proclaim, on a personal and collective level, for those inside and outside the church, that sin and evil are real and destructive.

Sin and evil frequently express themselves in forms of power abuse. Yet we do not seem to have the power to stop it. In confession we are led to face our part in this abuse. As God's people, we cannot be idealists about any form of human power. We should be alert to the forces of darkness that use and abuse power, as well as such powers exercised by the people of God and the institution of the church. In turn, there is power in confessing this truth of our need.

When we offer the prayer of confession, we take power abuse seriously. We admit that we are both its victims and its perpetrators. We need to dwell in such confession honestly and ruthlessly. At the same time, we offer our prayer in the trust of God's power for redemption. So we pray trusting in the One who declares that the full scope of sin has been personally faced, battled and defeated by Jesus Christ. Sin does not have the final word, but it takes the power of Christ's life, death and resurrection to defeat evil and triumph over it. In that sense, it helps make us more realistic about the subtleties of power, its damage and its limits. We confess as those in need, who need to turn from our interests of power to see ourselves and our neighbors differently.

Confession is brutal and essential work. It is an expression of the power of the Holy Spirit's conviction and strength. In it we submit our central human crisis to the One who alone has the power to change us. This is part of what worship is for, and it is troubling that so many churches sidestep it at a time when power abuse is rampant in the world.

Declaration of Forgiveness and Assurance of Pardon

"There is therefore now no condemnation for those who are in Christ Jesus. For the law of the Spirit of life in Christ Jesus has set you free from the law of sin and of death. For God has done what the law, weakened by the flesh, could not do" (Romans 8:1-3). The true power that is stronger and more sufficient than any other is the Word of God, which is living, active and effective. The declaration of God's forgiveness is our assurance. This act of worship declares what God's power has accomplished. It says that in the face of our own deadend, hopeless recalcitrant reality, there is a greater power that has entered into our crisis and accomplished what we could not.

It assumes our resolve to live repentantly. This means to live in light of a realignment of power, between the individual and humanity and God. No one is free from the need for the saving grace of Jesus Christ. The incarnation, death and resurrection of Jesus and the gift of the Holy Spirit give us the power to live a life "to do justice, and to love kindness, / and to walk humbly with [our] God" (Micah 6:8). They give us what we are powerless to give ourselves: forgiveness. They satisfy God's heart for justice through his own love. The power given to us by God can be redeemed by God.

This gives us freedom to move out into the world as those who seek justice. It flows from the assurance that we do not proclaim or promote ourselves and that the hope we offer does not come from us. We have already acknowledged that we are complicit in actions that have contributed to suffering, and we know something of "having no hope and [being] without God in the world" (Ephesians 2:12):

> But God, who is rich in mercy, out of the great love with which he loved us even when we were dead through our trespasses, made us alive together with Christ—by grace you have been saved—and raised us up with him and seated us with him in the heavenly places in Christ Jesus, so that in the ages to come he might show the immeasurable riches of his grace in kindness toward us in Christ Jesus. For by grace you have been saved through faith, and this is not your own doing; it is the gift of God—not the result of works, so that no one may boast. For we are what he has made us, created in Christ Jesus for good works, which God prepared beforehand to be our way of life. (Ephesians 2:4-10)

Those good works are the trajectory of the forgiven and include all the signs of God's heart for justice.

Baptism

Baptism is a mark of our new identity, based not on the power of tribe or family, education or status, race or gender, but on the power of God's promises. This is the gift of an identity that bears the marks of God's saving power. Infant baptism especially conveys this—emphasizing that before we have the power to do anything, God's power is for us. Similarly, in adult baptism we enter into the death and resurrection of the One who alone has power to triumph over sin and death. God's power, evident in baptism, is the power both to promise and to be faithful, to create and re-create, to name and rename, to die and to rise.

Injustice is often an assertion of a false identity. This is what distorts vocation in the kidnapper, rapist, persecutor, power broker, controller, manipulator, subverter. These false identities are sustained by lies, especially about the legitimacy of their power. Baptism reorders that by naming our utter vulnerability and lack of self-qualification. It is about receiving what we cannot lay hold of, earn or demand. Baptism is a pure, undeserved gift. It comes from the only source of power that loves purely and freely and bathes us in love that washes and claims us.

The Rural Presbyterian Church in northern India is an indigenous church composed of the *dalit* ("untouchable") people. They are victims of a vile form of injustice known as the caste system. Though it is officially illegal, the caste culture still thrives and crushes the poorest of the people. By Hindu law, children of dalits can only be given a derogatory name at birth (e.g., stupid, ugly, dumb). But at the Rural Presbyterian Church when dalits come to faith in Jesus Christ, they have a renaming ceremony, which utterly relabels them in light of God's grace and mercy. They step into a new identity with a new name. This extraordinary gift shifts the power in every part of life.

This example of renaming expresses the core of what baptism affirms: that God, who creates and gives us our true identity, acts to reclaim us from all evil tyranny in and around us. Through the witness of God's people, we are claimed for an identity which is both present and future. Jesus came among us as an untouchable himself, in order that through him all of us who are untouchables might have abundant life. By baptism we are "God's chosen ones, holy and beloved" (Colossians 3:12), which is exactly what we need to remember and to live.

Lord's Supper

The power of the Lord's Supper, or the Eucharist, is the embodiment of the pure, serving, self-offering communion of the Father, Son and Spirit. At the Communion table, we are invited (again without any legitimacy of our own) to sit in fellowship with God—both with God (in his triune being) and with God's people (in the life of the church). The One whose power saved Israel, who is remembered and celebrated in the Passover Seder, who is now personally present in Jesus Christ, becomes our Passover. He stoops to wash our feet, not to be served but to serve. He offers us his body and his blood as a sign of our belonging to him.

We are invited to eat and drink at this table with others who, like us, are not worthy to be there. We do not deserve to be invited, and we would not necessarily have chosen the others at the table with us. Still, Jesus Christ welcomes us to eat and drink at this table, remembering our need for the power of his cross and our anticipation of sharing one day in the heavenly banquet, when God's power will make all things new. The power of the lion lying down with the lamb is the power that removes all injustice and re-creates this and all true communion.

We sit at the Communion table with adulterers, child abusers, betrayers, deniers, coercers, liars. We also sit at the table with the destitute, the poor, the addicts, the illiterate, the depressed, the forgotten, the needy. In other words, we join those who are like us and unlike us. Everyone's abuse of power should, of course, keep us from the table, but not when it is presided over by the One who came to seek and save the lost. The One with all power takes the towel, stoops and washes our feet. This is the clearest form of restructuring power in a world of broken and deceptive power.

If this were not enough, this same Host takes the cup of salvation and says, "This is my body that is for you. Do this in remembrance of me. . . . This cup is the new covenant in my blood. . . . Do this . . . in remembrance of me" (1 Corinthians 11:24-25). Keep doing it. Come again and again. And every time you do so, remember him. Remember that you have been bought with a price. Your life is no longer your own. You belong to God in Christ. This strips away false power and affirms and reorders life-giving power. This is the Eucharist that witnesses to the power of life.

It is on the basis of this upside-down expression of love that the universe is to be grounded. It is on the basis of this love that all power is judged and held accountable. It is on the basis of this love that all accounts will be settled. It is a love so great that not only will it be just, it will be nonviolent, self-offering, satisfied. It is the power to sit at the table and serve, love and give power away to those who might betray and deny you. It is the power to lay your power aside. It is the power to bring people together in a fellowship that is not about their power but about the Servant's power. It is the power of agape love: "Forgive them; for they do not know what they are doing" (Luke 23:34). We need this love in order to give it away as we seek justice.

When members of my congregation come forward to receive Communion, I can easily get lost in their faces. We are such an unlikely lot. We are from different backgrounds, races, needs and experiences. We know human power is broken: we have seen and tasted that. Yet we have also tasted and seen that the Lord is good. We are desperate to know the power of God's love and justice more deeply. We are also figuring out how this table fellowship rewrites our guest lists, reformulates our priorities and recasts our common life.

The passing of the peace, which often accompanies the Eucharist, is an expression of living out the unity and peace of the gospel with one another in the body of Christ. When the worship services in my church allow time for this, I have been amazed at how rich and important the practice can be. It is a way of acknowledging and acting on the need to be right with each other in the body of Christ. In some ways, it is like a dress rehearsal for going out and extending the peace of Christ to the world.

Singing and Music

Singing is one of the more physical elements in worship services. As such, it is a distinct expression of physical power. But music is first and foremost an expression of emotional power. That is why it can meet us in and take us to places like nothing else can. Music both embodies and disciplines power. From the jail at Philippi to the Birmingham jail, God's people have known that worshipful singing, especially in the face of injustice, is one of the strongest acts of faith, hope and love available to us.

Our worship services do not need to be near prisons for singing to remind us of the liberating power of music to describe, name, feel, hear and cry out about injustice and to call forth our trust in God. Whether it is a song of lament or a spiritual, a note of joy or a cry of anguish, music helps give voice to some of our deepest struggles like nothing else can.

In the midst of a world of suffering and need, we sing. We enter into the longings and laments of God and thereby share God's heart. We do this for the sake of enlarging the context and perspective we live in. Music can express joy, beauty, complexity, history—of a certain people or the world—with struggles and with hope. Music embodies critical elements of our lives and of our call to do justice. So justice is not a Gnostic dream but an embodied, physical experience.

Spirituals and gospel songs open our hearts in empathy and identification. When we hear or sing such music, what may be objective ("people suffer") becomes subjective ("we suffer"). The whole exercise of making such music can instruct, motivate and renew our response to suffering in the world.

Music can be a bold enactment of some of the same elements that doing justice demands, and it gives us emotional practice in naming and describing what our life and call should be. We can easily become overwhelmed by injustice. Music can reawaken our voice, ignite our righteous anger, intensify our conviction, strengthen our resolve. It is all about laying hold of power we are meant to exercise as citizens of another kingdom.

Something happens when God's people sing. This is a time in our culture when music is so often about public performance and watching while others sing. But something extraordinary can happen in our lives when we use our own voices to reach up toward God through music. In our church some of the most powerful moments of being visited by God happen when we make our musical response to the Word that has been proclaimed. In the notes, the words, the silence, we offer our hearts and minds to God. And we are changed and called.

God's Word Read Aloud

All human power is derived from the God who speaks. Any word on our tongues is created, and ultimately given its boundary, by the Word of God. We are only actors in the world—good, bad or indifferent—because God spoke creation into existence and began its redemption through the Living Word, Jesus Christ. No human word exists outside of this Word.

Life and worship is a response to this Word. As human beings, we may foolishly consider ourselves independent from God. But that is a lie. Forgetting or denying God is profoundly destructive to knowing ourselves and each other.

Scripture offers us God's purpose for and his response to our human condition. Scripture comes to us as the record of an oral word, an address by God to the community of faith. When we stop speaking and actually listen to the reading of the Bible in worship, we are attending to that Word on which our choices and actions are to be based. We listen for instruction, encouragement, correction, clarity, wisdom and more. Together we listen to the authority and power to which we are accountable. This is not God's op-ed, just another opinion piece in an ocean of voices. It is the Word of Life.

Again, to listen well to Scripture is an exercise in laying down power. As we hear God's Word, we are redefined, challenged and redirected in our use of power. All other powers in the world are set in this context. This ancient Word, by the living power of the Holy Spirit, speaks authoritatively into our lives by its mere reading. It is a Word about life and hope in the face of all of humanity's greatest problems. It is full of God's response in speech and action to evil and injustice in the world. And it is God's intended means to call forth, equip and commission his people to live in service of him.

In the biblical narrative, power is not handled like we might expect. This is why we have the "problem of evil": If God is all good and all powerful, why does evil exist? While this question is not directly raised in the Bible, Bible-reading and theologically minded and justice-oriented people have always asked it. The Bible clearly indicates that God takes evil with such seriousness it ultimately leads to the greatest act of personal engagement and sacrifice: the cross. In humility and frustration, generations of people have seen this as grounds for hope as well as grounds for admitting to a mystery.

The cross is our greatest comfort and the clearest sign that God's way of dealing with power, sin and injustice is not our way. We hear this again and again as we let Scripture talk. In the end, God's power will establish *shalom*. All will be held accountable. Justice will be fully served. All will be well. In the meantime, Scripture tells us to trust, love, sacrifice, lay down power, live a life worthy of the gospel, work while it is yet day! As we hear and learn all this, we are to remember and imitate the life and ministry of Jesus, who emptied himself for our sake and calls us to do likewise.

The faithful hearing of the Word of God read aloud depends on the commitment of those who plan worship services and who preach to see that a Scripture-rich diet is offered to all who gather in worship. Using the Common Lectionary as the basis for the weekly Scripture readings has the benefit of enabling worshipers to encounter the full range of Scripture's themes, not just those that are chosen by chance or are our personal favorites. Themes of injustice and power abuse are embedded in many Bible texts, so we should watch for them even when the primary point may be something else. Over the course of a year, worship should also feature preaching that is especially devoted to books of Scripture or a topical series in which justice themes are more fully and vigorously explored.

After fifteen years of planning and two years of construction, our church was preparing to dedicate our new facilities. I planned a series of sermons for that time period that would take us through Philippians. The long building process challenged our relationship with the city of Berkeley in addition to challenging us to stay on track with our mission and ministry objectives without getting diverted by the time and expenses. This was no small feat, and God was faithful. We wrestled with whether our money should have been spent otherwise, not least on issues of local or international justice. The leadership of our congregation took those issues seriously and concluded that the purpose of these new educational facilities was primarily to equip our congregation for the next century (Lord willing) of outreach.

On the dedication Sunday, the text for the sermon was Philippians 2:5-11. The message centered on our call to ministry, and the worship service itself was about dedicating our lives to the mission of God. During the sermon, each person in the congregation received a wooden cross made of chwa wood, just like the one Daniel had shown me in the camp in northern Uganda. As I preached through Philippians 2:5-11, we focused on the cross as God's central act of showing his power. The only way our lives—or our church's new facilities—could make any sense in the kingdom of God or be avenues of grace in the world was this: if we lived in such a way that the cross enables who we are and what we do in Berkeley to tie us deeply and irrevocably to Daniel and others like him. Only then, when the power God has given us accomplishes that, will our worship express the cross's power to redefine every other power and to create God's one true communion. Our mission depends on our worship.

God's Word Preached

This is where the force of God's Word read aloud is expressed though the personality and wisdom of the preacher, who seeks to expose God's people to that Word for the sake of their personal and collective transformation and mission. This is all about power and powerlessness.

The "folly" of preaching is itself a sign of God's peculiar expression of power. But for the grace of God, preaching would simply be the ludicrous act of a finite, ordinary, sinful (but gifted and called) individual expounding from Scripture and speaking on God's behalf to people who are just as finite, ordinary and sinful. It is so unlikely. So ordinary. So typical of God's personal character and surprising means. It is Moses before Pharaoh, David before Goliath, Jesus before Herod. It is God purposing to do what is needed through jars of clay.

Preachers stand not on their own authority or on their own words, but only in service to the power and authority of God, who is beyond even the most eloquent, most impassioned or the most powerful personality. The preached Word can effectively deliver God's message to the people for today. It is also our testimony to a God who does not need us but who uses us by his power and grace. It's the invitation that all God's ambassadors have the privilege of offering in Jesus' name: "Follow me." This is the power that is changing the world.

My own experiences make the folly of preaching so evident. I trust that God has given me gifts, and I try to use them faithfully. But what grips me far more is that the only hope that transformation will happen is if God is truly in it. It can only be accomplished if the mercy of Jesus Christ by the power of the Holy Spirit is actually at work. Before I preach I pray because my weakness is so evident to me. Then I lift my head and look into the faces of the people I know and love. I stand before them utterly inadequate to give what we all need most: a Word from God. I try to unpack the Scripture in a way that will expose its meaning. I try to point in the direction of its implications, challenges, awkwardnesses, questions and demands.

Sociologically speaking, preaching is an example of human power: one person speaks and everyone else listens. But spiritually speaking it's about the weakness of a human agent and the grace of God's presence by Word and Spirit in the community. It's about God's Word confronting the power in my life. Only then does it seem to work in the lives of others. I have to look into the faces of those who have power in my life, both for good and ill. I have to hear the Word and seek to declare it out of obedience to God, not out of a desire to please my congregation. I have to let the truth of the Word do its work in me at the points of my greatest need, especially if I want to release the Word to do likewise in the lives of those who hear me preach. It can only be God's gift if the links are made, if the conviction comes, if my own powers are rightly reordered and restored. When this happens, God's power does what I so clearly cannot.

Intercessory Prayer

In prayer we lay ourselves out before God in honesty and dependence. We dare to talk to God, speaking or silent. This is not a right but a gift.

This is conversation with the One who holds all power in the palm of his hand. In Washington, D.C., it is said that power is measured by access. Prayer is all about access to the God who reigns over all.

Prayer is also the integration of coming in our dependence, weakness, finitude and longing, asking for God's power to do what we need, for our sake and the sake of others. Prayer is taking God's invitation to personal relationship at face value. It's neither formulaic nor predictable. It is relationship. It's not about our power but about God's.

In prayer we bring the wreckage of human power to God. We have too much or too little. We need to have it redefined and recontextualized. Often we don't realize how true this is until we try to articulate it to God. In prayer we practice being powerless, and we seek God's power for the powerless people we name. It is as though we are claiming and extending power into lives and places, circumstances and relationships where that power can really make a difference. Whether we who pray have the power of kings or keys, of money or might, we seek the power of God for those in need.

I'm convinced that the dynamic life of the congregation I serve is explained by God's grace answering the humble prayers of ordinary believers who seek God's blessing for all we do. That is the story of power and prayer. I am utterly dependent on the way the prayers of such saints have changed my life and ministry. I think the same is true of our whole church. We are what we are by the grace of God at work through the prayers of these saints who lean on God for our sake and for the sake of all we long to see happen in our ministry, both locally and globally.

Offering

We offer all we are in response to all that God has revealed himself to be. In joy, hope and sacrifice, we lay down our lives and our gifts, acknowledging the claim of God on our lives. In freedom, without divine coercion, we place our gifts—that is to say, everything—in God's hands. In season and out of season, in times of ease and times of difficulty, we worship by making our offering.

The offering of money, which is significantly the kind of offering we tend to think of most often and is itself a sign of power, presents us with a key moment in our worship. Here is one of the great power collisions in worship. We live in a culture that worships money and neglects or forgets God. We are meant to live worshiping God and slaying the idols in our lives—including money. When the time for the offering comes each week, the practice helps us remember what belongs to us and what doesn't, helps us understand what the sabbath does to stewardship of all that we have.

It is not a cheap way of buying off our conscience or buying God's love. It's meant to be an act of surrendering our first fruits and facing down the power of money, status, achievement, self-absorption. In the offering we practice turning over power. That is a good thing. Of course, it should be done wisely, but it should still be done! It should be done purposefully, but it should be done! It should be done generously, but it should be done!

Defeating the power of money in our lives is part of defeating false power in every area. Jesus says more about the power of money than almost any other spiritual danger, so it is a particularly important issue if we are to go out into the world and be free to live trusting God's power, not our own.

Commissioning and Benediction

The end of the Gospel of Matthew is remarkable. This Gospel has much to say about the power of the kingdom of God and how the twelve apostles are the type for the new Israel. These details are precisely what make Matthew 28 so stunning, not least in what it says about God's vision of power. The text simply says, "Now the eleven disciples went to Galilee, to the mountain to which Jesus had directed them. When they saw him, they worshiped him; but some doubted" (vv. 16-17).

It's eleven disciples, not twelve. And they are believing doubters. This group is fewer and weaker than the "new Israel" paradigm would have implied. It's not about those who have been strong, vigorous, competent, true believers. Yet it is to these eleven believing and doubting followers that Jesus gives the Great Commission: "All authority in heaven and on earth has been given to me. Go therefore and make disciples of all nations" (Matthew 28:18-19). This is an unexpected redefinition of power.

Every time I say the charge and benediction at the end of the service, I think of this moment in Matthew's Gospel, and I take heart. We are sent out, like the apostles, fewer and weaker than we might have been, but exactly the ones God wants to use. What I say in essence is this: "So go out and live the life of those who worship God, exercising the passion of Christ in humble power that seeks justice, loves mercy and walks humbly with our God. Live in a way that entirely redefines the meaning of power in the world, and you will be blessed to be a blessing. Do this, and you will show you have been with God and that God has been with you. 'For the one who is in you is greater than the one who is in the world' (1 John 4:4)."

We are sent out for the sake of another kingdom, in the name and power of Someone else, for the sake of the powerless and the forgotten. Jesus is Lord. So it really is all about worship that does justice, worship that realigns power.

8 Dwelling in Exodus or in Exile?

WHEN I FIRST CAME TO BERKELEY TO INTERVIEW FOR THE position in university ministry, my guide drove me past Memorial Stadium on the campus of the University of California. Rather nonchalantly she said, "This is where one of the major earthquake fault lines is. In fact, it cuts right under the stadium." Surprised, I asked, "And we're all OK with this?" For someone unfamiliar with living in earthquake territory, this casual observation sounded stunning! Even twenty-five years later I still remember how it struck me. But to my host, living near a fault line had long since become commonplace. Life was defined by a fault line. But absent an earthquake, it was a fault line without drama.

Since then I have learned that life in the Bay Area is constantly affected by these fault lines (e.g., building codes, laws, costs, wall cracks, lawsuits, earthquake-preparedness drills, etc.), but at the same time the residents live in denial that "the Big One" will ever occur. Both things say a lot about how life is lived in the Bay Area.

Two fault lines exist in the biblical narrative that both define the drama of God's relationship with Israel and shape God's relationship with the church today: the exodus and the exile. Each paradigm still has great force in locating God's people in the world. They are relevant here because the "promised land" mentality of American culture and Christianity has given dramatic play to the exodus paradigm but has muffled the exile paradigm. Americans are always ready for the promised land but have far less readiness to face the more ambiguous and demanding life of exile.

In both paradigms we see God's heart for injustice. In Egypt it is God's concern for the injustice Israel suffers. In Babylon it is God's concern for the injustice Israel has perpetrated. Both are still relevant to our understanding of God's purposes in the world.

Life in Egypt

This long and defining period in Israel's history picks up the pilgrim theme that begins when God calls Abraham to move to Ur. Eventually Abraham's descendants come to live in Egypt. By the time of the Exodus, Israel has been living within the paradigm of slavery for four hundred years.

> Now a new king arose over Egypt, who did not know Joseph. He said to his people, "Look, the Israelite people are more numerous and more powerful than we. Come, let us deal shrewdly with them, or they will increase and, in the event of war, join our enemies and fight against us and escape from the land." Therefore they set taskmasters over them to oppress them with forced labor. They built supply cities, Pithom and Rameses, for Pharaoh. But the more they were oppressed, the more they multiplied and spread, so that the Egyptians came to dread the Israelites. The Egyptians became ruthless in imposing tasks on the Israelites, and made their lives bitter with hard service in mortar and brick and in every kind of field labor. They were ruthless in all the tasks that they imposed on them. (Exodus 1:8-14)

Egypt was the oppressor, Israel was the oppressed. Israel's goal was to be delivered from the tyranny of Egypt, to get away from their oppressors and into the Promised Land. The story has a clear definition and direction. The plot requires miracles to move forward, but the trajectory of the story is getting out of Egypt and getting to the land "flowing with milk and honey."

This context sets the stage for the call of Moses, the revelation of God's name to his people, the deliverance of Israel from Egypt, the giving of the Law and the wandering of God's people in the wilderness for forty years. These events define Israel's core identity, setting the terms and the location of their common life as Yahweh's people. We cannot make sense of Israel's life, past or present, without this dramatic story and God's promises and provisions along the way.

> Then the LORD said, "I have observed the misery of my people who are in Egypt; I have heard their cry on account of their taskmasters. Indeed, I know their sufferings, and I have come down to deliver them from the Egyptians, and to bring them up out of that land to a good and broad land, a land flowing with milk and honey, to the country of the Canaanites, the Hittites, the Amorites, the Perizzites, the Hivites, and the Jebusites. The cry of the Israelites has now come to me; I have also seen how the Egyptians oppress them. So come, I will send you to Pharaoh to bring my people, the Israelites, out of Egypt." But Moses said to God, "Who am I that I should go to Pharaoh, and bring the Israelites out of Egypt?" He said, "I will be with you; and this shall be the sign for you that it is I who sent you: when you have brought the people out of Egypt, you shall worship God on this mountain." (Exodus 3:7-12)

The New Testament picks up on this theme of captivity and exodus to describe the work of salvation and liberation that God accomplishes for Gentile as well as Jew through Jesus Christ. Our human condition means we dwell in darkness and we need to be set free by the light of the gospel of Jesus Christ. We are captive to ourselves and to the petty, self-centered obsessions we attend to so often. We are captive to sin and death. We need to be born again, passing from death to life, in order to enter into the kingdom of God and find our true freedom. This exodus is our hope. Jesus Christ leads us out of bondage and into life.

Therefore, brothers and sisters, holy partners in a heavenly calling, consider that Jesus, the apostle and high priest of our confession, was faithful to the one who appointed him, just as Moses also "was faithful in all God's house." Yet Jesus is worthy of more glory than Moses, just as the builder of a house has more honor than the house itself. (For every house is built by someone, but the builder of all things is God.) Now Moses was faithful in all God's house as a servant, to testify to the things that would be spoken later. Christ, however, was faithful over God's house as a son, and we are his house if we hold firm the confidence and the pride that belong to hope. (Hebrews 3:1-6)

This is the heart of the good news. It is not just Israel who lived in bondage, but humanity in general. Coming to know Jesus Christ is stepping into the liberty that only the Lord can give. "For freedom Christ has set us free. . . . Do not submit again to a yoke of slavery" (Galatians 5:1). Paul's movement beyond even captivity to "the Law" ushers in a new day under the rule of God's grace in Christ (who has satisfied and fulfilled the Law) that is the kingdom of God.

This exodus theme has rightly had a profound impact on the church over its two-thousand-year history. We must acknowledge the particular prominence and influence the exodus paradigm has had in the life of the American church. After all, the United States was established by those who were leaving various kinds of bondage to pursue religious and spiritual freedom. It was their own exodus to these shores. The westward expansion of the United States, and with it, the church, was also an exodus, a pursuit of the promised land. Each settlement along the way was placing a stake in the promised land of that area. This is at the core of American culture. Frequently it was linked to a sense of God's intervention, divine destiny and special provision.

The appeal of this optimistic, past-and-future, leaving-from and going-toward paradigm of the exodus defines a great deal of American culture. It is biblically prominent, emotionally attractive, socially productive and personally hopeful. It is influential in both secular and Christian culture. It has joined with American pragmatism to create a social environment in which some feel the gospel of America and the gospel of the Bible have become fused.

Christians in the United States live and hear the gospel in an exodus-shaped culture. A great deal of social and political rhetoric reflects a fairly simple binary approach to the world; people think they know the good guys from the bad guys and identify themselves with one or the other. All this, despite the atrocities committed against Native Americans during the "conquest" of North America. All this, despite the fact that the vestiges of battles over slavery and civil rights are still with us today.

Everyone wants the promised land, so we push on, as individuals or as a community or as a nation. We know which side we are on. We think we know who is on the other side, and we are determined to set things right. This attitude undergirds our hearing of the gospel and our sense of place in relation to other nations and peoples. The rich economic and social inheritances that are part of the American consciousness make it easy for many to suppose we are in the promised land. It can make us suppose that we are the called, the chosen, the blessed.

God's deliverance of Israel comes from seeing the suffering of his people at the unjust and cruel hands of their Egyptian taskmasters. He delivers and sets them free. The unidirectional narrative means once Egypt is behind them, Egypt might as well not be. Israel doesn't go back to Egypt to enact justice. Once Israel has left injustice behind, that tyranny is no longer in view. Their concern was not injustice per se, but their own experience of oppression.

Put this way, the exodus paradigm exposes the temptation that Israel had, and that the contemporary church shares, to give in to our instinct to escape. Appropriate exodus does involve leaving something behind and moving ahead. However, when it becomes an excuse for entitlement, rejection, judgment, disconnection, and deliberate and pervasive forgetfulness, it fosters a lifestyle of running away that undermines both true worship and true justice. A vigorous theology of worship that encounters the living God of heaven and earth is never escapist. It's never about forgetting the neighbor, not least the neighbor who is blind and poor, or oppressed and hungry. It is about never submitting again to the wrong yoke of slavery but instead taking on the rightful yoke of Jesus, whose burden is light.

Consider how our selective memory contributes to devastating escapism. Like Israel, the church in the United States tends to see the gifts of God's blessing as the sign of a special anointing rather than a call to responsibility. God's blessing is given so that we become a blessing, not so that we get more and more blessing. Israel often forgot this, and so does the American church. We remember what we want to remember, and we forget what we find cumbersome or problematic. God's deliverance of Israel was intended to cultivate an empathy and mercy toward others who are enslaved. In the imagery of Jesus' parable, the overwhelming generosity of the master was intended to be shown in the servant's generosity toward others. But like Israel and like the servant, we don't do what God intends. This is forgetting where we truly live. Exodus becomes a mode of escape instead of deliverance.

Listen again to this parable of the unforgiving servant in Matthew 18:23-35:

> For this reason the kingdom of heaven may be compared to a king who wished to settle accounts with his slaves. When he began the reckoning, one who owed him ten thousand talents was brought to him; and, as he could not pay, his lord ordered him to be sold, together with his wife and children and all his possessions, and payment to be made. So the slave fell on his knees before him,

saying, "Have patience with me, and I will pay you everything." And out of pity for him, the lord of that slave released him and forgave him the debt. But that same slave, as he went out, came upon one of his fellow slaves who owed him a hundred denarii; and seizing him by the throat, he said, "Pay what you owe." Then his fellow slave fell down and pleaded with him, "Have patience with me, and I will pay you." But he refused; then he went and threw him into prison until he would pay the debt. When his fellow slaves saw what had happened, they were greatly distressed, and they went and reported to their lord all that had taken place. Then his lord summoned him and said to him, "You wicked slave! I forgave you all that debt because you pleaded with me. Should you not have had mercy on your fellow slave, as I had mercy on you?" And in anger his lord handed him over to be tortured until he would pay his entire debt. So my heavenly Father will also do to every one of you, if you do not forgive your brother or sister from your heart.

The unforgiving servant gets the blessing, but fails to translate that into the call to bless someone else facing need. It's an easy tendency just to receive and not give in return. We usually lean toward selfishness as human beings. Where I live, for example, the tales of the Califormia gold rush were surpassed by the tales of dot-com boom. It has become the stuff of contemporary legend, and it bears the marks of our endless appetite for more and better promised lands, seldom sharing the bounty or seeking the promised land for others.

The assumption seems to be that as long as we desire more, we must not have reached the promised land yet! It's true of course that God's full blessing is not yet complete. This means that we are still in the process of exodus, we are still in the wilderness, we are still living daily by the manna of God's provision and looking back with joy and gratitude. Consumerism is partly an indicator of our voracious appetite for all to be well. We buy and keep buying because we are trying to make it to a promised land where there is no hunger anymore—for ourselves. Consumerism, however, is an unsatisfying well. It never accomplishes what it offers. But in our culture, there seems to be nowhere else to turn with our hunger, so we go back to it again and again. Our hearts are restless because they have not truly found their rest in God.

We are caught in a secular exodus of consumer frenzy trying to acquire the promised land. In the end, all we have is more stuff—not more blessing. We try to escape from the responsibility of loving and serving those who have less. The distance between ourselves and the poor becomes greater. The lessons we were meant to remember and embody in acts of compassion, mercy and love toward those in the heart of God devolve into occasional acts of charity, giving at the office or tax-deductible contributions. This kind of giving is more of a compartmentalized action with positive tax consequences than the overflow of generosity that comes from a sacrificial offering of the heart. While the two things can go together, sadly the former often trumps the latter.

When members of American churches give on average just 2 or 3 percent of their income, it doesn't seem like we understand our wealth or blessing. Our response should be more like that of Matthew the tax collector, our lives turned upside down because of the extravagant mercy and deliverance of God that offers us the promised land of new life in Christ. Our generosity should be more like that of the Macedonian church, commended by the apostle Paul; even in their "extreme poverty," they still "gave according to their means, and even beyond their means," begging Paul for "the privilege of sharing" in the offering for the Jerusalem church (2 Corinthians 8:2-4).

Our culture claims the promise and avoids the pain. This produces a slumbering church that fails to heed God's call to worship that does justice. We don't want to lay down our lives or take up our cross daily. As

Jesus said, the risk in doing so is that we gain the whole world but lose our own soul (Mark 8:36).

The smugly held exodus paradigm has no place for worry about issues of justice. Such things are of no concern if you are "just a passin' through." What matters is getting beyond the wilderness to obtain the benefits of the promised land. There is a transient quality to everything else. The poor, the naked, the forgotten are left behind in the forward progress of pursuing God's blessing. Injustice is just a fault line without drama, as long as the Big One doesn't shake middle-class Americans.

American Christian culture often communicates to people around the world, "You should just seek God's promised land, like we have, and then you can have what we have!" This is a broad miscalculation of where humanity dwells, and it daily damages the mission of Jesus Christ.

It is important to note that this tendency plays out differently in the African American church than it does in the white American church. The exodus is a central part of liberation theology, whether for African Americans or others. Those who live in circumstances in which the greatest hope is for deliverance naturally connect with the narrative of the exodus. To those in the African American church, for whom issues of injustice are still daily concerns, the exodus story speaks to the deepest longings for deliverance. The promised land is both now and in eternity, expressed and embodied as the land of justice.

In the dominant culture, however, the hope of the promised land in the exodus paradigm is a more powerful attraction than the deliverance from injustice. This difference in appropriating the exodus themes of Old and New Testament speaks powerfully of our invisible assumptions, but we simply do not see it in our sleepwalking lives.

Life in Babylon

In contrast to the exodus paradigm, the exile paradigm is quite complex. Though Israel has obviously become the oppressed, they are being judged by God for being oppressors themselves. Babylon, the epitome of injustice and corrupt power, is now used by God to discipline God's people. Israel is not victimized by Babylon as it was by Egypt. In the exile Israel is fully implicated in its own subjugation. Those outside Israel are used to discipline God's people as God calls them to live like they are meant to live. God's promise to Abraham and his line—to be blessed to be a blessing—now faces a different, more complex grace—to be judged (in exile) in order to become a blessing (in exile).

The exile encompasses the disorienting horrors of the demise of Israel, the fall of Jerusalem, the desecration of the temple and the captivity of God's people in Babylon. All of this comes as a consequence of God's judgment on his people, not just as a result of Babylon's own aggression. No wonder they lament in depression and sorrow, "Our captors / asked us for songs, / and our tormentors asked for mirth, saying, / 'Sing us one of the songs of Zion!'" (Psalm 137:3), for Zion was no more.

Israel's call in exile is to work out what it means to dwell in a foreign land and yet live like those who belong to Yahweh. The challenge is to demonstrate the distinctive character of righteousness and justice that shows where they truly live, even when every force of assimilation is upon them. What Israel had been called to do but failed at in Jerusalem, it must now learn to do in Babylon. They must do so for their own sake as well as the sake of their oppressors.

As the story is presented in the book of Daniel, Nebuchadnezzar is determined to breed conformity—in names, language, literature, food and the whole way of life of Babylon. Meanwhile Daniel and his friends remember that though they live in the house of the king, they are dedicated to live first before the God who is King over all. By remembering that, they live with astonishing freedom, courage and boldness. They are unhooked from the assumptions and the system that has taken them hostage.

The challenge for Israel in exile is not to escape. Their vocation is not to get out. It is to stay and be changed by seeking the welfare of their enemy: "Seek the [shalom] of the city where I have sent you into exile . . . for in its [shalom] you will find your [shalom]" (Jeremiah 29:7).

There are impressive Christian leaders in the Majority World[1] who strike me as modern-day Daniels. They are among the best and the brightest of their nations. They could leave their homes, go someplace where their intelligence, education and skills would be well compensated. They could choose to go to the promised land. Instead, having received many blessings themselves, they decide to stay in their own land and contribute all they can to the life of their country. Uganda, Malaysia, Malawi, Indonesia, Central African Republic, Chad—these are places where life is much harder, especially if the goal is a promised land rather than embracing the challenges of exile.

The New Testament sees exilic qualities as being descriptive of the church's life as well. We are living in a compromised setting as strangers in a strange land. We are in but not of the world. We live in the midst of an "already and not yet" transition. It is here in the world, precisely where Jesus prayed we would be, that we are to live "worthy of the gospel" and "work out [our] own salvation" (Philippians 1:27; 2:12). Peter also writes:

> Beloved, I urge you as aliens and exiles to abstain from the desires of the flesh that wage war against the soul. Conduct yourselves honorably among the Gentiles, so that, though they malign you as evildoers, they may see your honorable deeds and glorify God when he comes to judge.
>
> For the Lord's sake accept the authority of every human institution, whether of the emperor as supreme, or of governors, as sent by him to punish those who do wrong and to praise those who do right. For it is God's will that by doing right you should silence the ignorance of the foolish. As servants of God, live as free people, yet

do not use your freedom as a pretext for evil. Honor everyone. Love the family of believers. Fear God. Honor the emperor. (1 Peter 2:11-17)

We give to Caesar what belongs to Caesar and to God what belongs to God (Matthew 22:21). Only in humble community do we have some chance of successfully distinguishing one from the other. We are to live as God's "peculiar" people, showing in our daily lives the dual citizenship that is ours. Like Israel, however, we usually fail to do this.

It's no great stretch to suggest that the American church is in exile in its own contemporary Babylon. Whether conservative or liberal, the church mostly looks like the culture around us. We are for the most part indistinguishable. We have decided to enjoy our Babylon while nodding occasionally to the God we say we worship. The life of the American church provides a type of religious window dressing for our culture. Most mainstream Christians quietly reject the strident tactics of culture war advocated by fundamentalists while also quietly living out the desire to not stand out at all. We just seek our own welfare and call it God's blessing, trying to offend as few people as possible along the way.

While we are highly attuned to avoid a faithful peculiarity that might offend, we also avoid a faithful peculiarity that might redeem. While we run from what might cause cultural or personal offense, we opt for benign acceptance of so many things that grieve our Lord Jesus Christ. The power that defines us is not the power of God we meet and know through worship; it's the social power of being "normal," accepted, popular, tolerant. We are defined by the economic power of our acumen, our education, our track record or our capacity to increase the bottom line. We are defined by Babylon, not by the cross.

Our unwillingness to live as faithful exiles explains our capacity to chase culture rather than transform it. It explains the sweeping compass of the worship wars that have preoccupied the church for the last decade while national and global problems go unattended. During a time that has been one of the most redefining periods in national and international history in years, the American church has done little to show that it truly seeks "the welfare of the city." While many Christians rue various economic concerns that impinge on our capacity to earn, the church has been inert in its concerns for the widening gap between the rich and the poor, in its outreach to the millions dying of HIV/AIDS, in its response to the burgeoning global sex-trafficking trade, in the ongoing decay and violence of our inner cities. Some crises (Hurricane Katrina, for example) do serve to remind us of profound economic and racial injustices in our nation, but the American church has only vaguely roused itself. Meanwhile, churches argue over whether the right praise music is used or whether the aesthetics of worship meet their emotional needs.

Is this the description of a church that is living in God in the world, one that is living as faithful exiles? It is far more complicated to live as exiles than to live as those in exodus. In exile we have to put down roots, plant gardens, build schools, read the newspaper, vote, advocate, serve and engage our world in countless ways. We have to do justice. We have to consider how to be faithful stewards of the resources God has given us. We have to do these things if we are in exile. But do we even know that we are in exile?

Dual Dimensions

Once again we see that *how* we live is an expression of *where* we live. If we think we live in exodus, life is all about getting to the promised land we think we deserve and desire. On the other hand, if we think we live in exile, then life's agenda is all about living distinctly where we are and determining whether our home in God or in "Babylon" will influence us most.

Jesus calls us to both domains of life. Both exodus and exile are God's intention. Both are to be our experience. Both are needed, and both have meaning. Both are to be a part of our daily living, and it takes both to make the fullest sense of God's purposes and plans. Both are spiritual and both are material, but in different ways. Worship and justice are needed in both dimensions. But if we think we are living in only one or the other of these paradigms and fail to see that we are to live in both, it will dramatically affect how we invest in justice and what we hope for.

For example, if I think I am only to live in the exodus paradigm, my sense of life is about getting through and getting out. I am not looking for intrinsic value or purposes in the people, places or things around me because "this world is not my home, I'm just a passin' through." Worship in the exodus dimension is living in profound gratitude that you have been set free—free to live with God and for God, free from captivity, darkness, despair, enslavement. Worship in the exile dimension means practicing our peculiar identity every day, "seek[ing] the welfare of the city, . . . for in its welfare, you will find your welfare" (Jeremiah 29:7).

You don't have to look long into the face of David, a young Kenyan man, to see bright and unusual joy. His story makes that joy all the more powerful. David was in the wrong place at the wrong time when a cruel policeman in Nairobi arrested him and shot him in the hand and wrist, which had to be amputated. In the midst of this ordeal, he was wrongfully detained and faced false charges that put his life at risk. God delivered David through the investigations and advocacy of the International Justice Mission. Not only was David set free, his oppressor was brought to justice. What's more, confident of God's grace in his life, David is now on course to become an attorney in Kenya so he can be an advocate for the vulnerable and the abused. David knows about both exodus and exile, which has led him into worship and out into doing justice.

Worship is the daily remembrance that the nightmare is over and that today is the joyful day of salvation. In the larger sense too, it is now in Christ a deliverance that is sure, if not complete. It's not the full, unfiltered worship of Zion, let alone of the day when the Lamb will open the seals of the book of life, but it is living life in God full of wonder for God's amazing grace.

Justice in exodus is the courage to name the bondages of life, to acknowledge the darkness and suffering, to be prepared to name the injustices for what they are, to confront Pharoah, to have the courage in faith not to be intimidated and to do so for the sake of telling the truth as well as for the hope of deliverance. It's about putting our hope in the God who hears the cries of the suffering and will not leave them or forsake them.

In exile, worship is claiming daily the identity that is in jeopardy, cultivating practices that help remind us where we came from and where we are going. Worship is the offering of ourselves to serve our neighbor (who may also be our enemy) because we are serving the God who promises to sustain us. It clarifies and grounds our lives in wisdom about what matters most (faithfulness to God) in a culture that demands we bow before a worldly king (idolatry in action). Worship does not remove us from exile, but it shapes how we live there. It tells us that time, gifts, abilities, opportunities, relationships and work all matter—if they become an offering to the One who alone truly deserves it.

Justice in exile involves a willingness to stand at the intersection of Babylon and God's kingdom and to practice the difference between honor and worship, submission and allegiance. If we understand that exilic living means staying instead of leaving, then we realize we are supposed to make a difference and seek the coming of God's kingdom on earth. If we are living in "exodus" while "exile" is thrown in our faces every day—at school or the office, at home, on the nightly news, wherever—we think those are all just distractions. But if we realize that we live in exile, then we can embrace all this as a part of the gift of God's call to be signposts, to be salt, to be light in the world. Exile allows us to hold on to the slow and steady path toward God's re-creation. We don't run toward exodus, but we hold on to the final outcome without falling prey to the hope of some easy spiritual escape.

For example, we won't be concerned about the environment if we think, *All this is going to burn up in the judgment anyway.* But if we think that we are called to live in a world that will not be destroyed but will be made new, with the continuity and discontinuity of life evidenced in the resurrection of Jesus, then we think differently about where we live. Creation will be fulfilled, not destroyed, in the new heaven and the new earth. That in turn changes *how* we live now. If our life is all about exodus, won't think about chronic, pervasive need and suffering. If the goal is getting through, not being "stupid" and making sure we are safe, we won't sacrifice for the sake of others. Jesus calls us to much more.

9 An Imagination for Justice

NO IMAGINATION RIVALS GOD'S. THE GOD WHO PUT THE "sliding shutter" on the lizard's eye and created more than three hundred kinds of hummingbirds has a boundless effluence of creativity. Each person bears God's signature and expresses that uniquely. Our God is Beauty, Goodness and Truth, and the fount from which all its many expressions come. The greatest evidence of this is the incarnation, life, death and resurrection of God. Here God's imagination is borne in mysterious, self-offering love that begins the re-creation of a fallen world that will one day become a new heaven and a new earth. Only God's imagination could dream such an end or fashion such a means.

By contrast, our imagination is crippled by evil. From the Garden onward, evil drives us to fixate on what is small and insignificant—to lose life, not gain it; to become people of small soul, not great. We fiddle with the petty. We are drawn into ever smaller appetites in the name of fashion, competition, power or addiction. Our world easily shrinks down to our size. Sin diminishes our ability to see, desire or imagine real goodness.

The human failure to pursue justice stems in part from a failure of imagination, an inability to see and be gripped by a vision of a world of justice. Why is this so lacking? It results from a world that forgets God and his vision. Within the church, safe worship impoverishes our imagination by failing to stimulate an impassioned imagination for the kingdom of God.

We desperately need worship that enlivens and enlarges our vision for seeking and doing justice. One of God's primary antidotes to our small-minded, human-bounded lives is the practice of cultivating a life that feeds from and imitates the imagination of God. This is one of the gifts that worship can give us. It is a telling cultural indictment that the church today is one of the last places people expect to see acts of imagination. At the same time, in a culture that often defines imagination by spectacle, God's people should be using their imaginations to put us in the vanguard of imaginative acts of love and justice.

One of my personal heroes is a man in our congregation named Arthur Ammann. Art was the first pediatric immunologist to diagnose an infant with HIV/AIDS. This changed Art's life. He immediately began to see the global implications of this discovery, and the comfortable life he had on the medical-school faculty of the University of California in San Francisco could not contain his heart or his imagination for responding to this pandemic. For the past thirty years, Art has given himself to the crisis of infants with HIV/AIDS. He has networked with small local clinics all over Africa to provide information, training and medicines aimed at preventing the transmission of HIV/AIDS from mothers to their babies. His spiritual imagination has expanded. His theological reflections have deepened. His personal courage and fierce determination have been tested. By God's grace, Art's imagination and heart drew him into science and toward people. For him, this was simply to follow the pathway of Jesus. From Art's example, our church has been drawn with him.

A worshipful imagination bears the mark of God's Spirit. Such imaginations for goodness would not be self-righteous, smug or small. Instead our imaginations would be vigorous and expansive—like God's, who is the source of such vision. In the real world we live in, such imagination seems pitifully and tragically infrequent. But it is the very nature of God's heart and mind. How do we cultivate an imagination for goodness? By living a lifestyle of worship. A lifestyle of worship lets God and God's dreams fill and guide us.

A New Environment

A God-renewed imagination is helped when we remember that by God's grace, the terms of life and of the world are set by God, who places us in the new environment of dwelling in his character and purposes.

Breathing the air. The only good thing about badly polluted air is that you can see it! But fresh air is invisible; it's intoxicatingly wonderful, but it is invisible and blows where it will. Part of living in the new environment of God's life in Christ is to be filled daily with the invisible fresh air of the Holy Spirit filling. This is really a call to spiritual practices that best allow us to breathe in the good air of God's grace.

We don't just "breathe" once a week on Sunday, whether we think we need it or not! We breathe continuously. Much of the social, mental and cultural air we breathe is polluted. We can survive on such air, but some of it is actually poisonous. To live a life of worship that does justice requires us to fill our lungs daily with the air of grace, divine compassion, wisdom and power. Doing justice in biblical terms does not arise from the will per se, nor from the heart of the activist who merely wants to "do" something. Doing justice is the effluence of breathing in the grace of God's mercy and justice toward us, and in his Spirit living justly in the world. It enlarges our imaginations and actions.

Prayer can be a great help in stimulating our imagination for the things of God. This means developing ongoing conversation with God about the people and events before you, about living beyond your own self-interest, about wanting God's heart of compassion and mercy for others. Praying for the ability to see empathetically gives us new vision. *Compassion* literally means "to suffer with," and prayer is one of the best ways we can grow in compassion. It involves standing in the presence of God, carrying the burdens of someone else.

Such prayer can also be difficult because it raises issues we don't like. Prayer can be hard, and apparently unanswered prayer can require discipline we may not readily have. Prayer may require us to face our theological doubts and longings. Prayer may cause us to face intractable evil. Prayer will lead us to times when we don't understand God or his ways. This is all part of identifying with the God who shares our burdens and carries our sorrows.

Rooted and grounded in love. Another part of our new environment is dwelling in God's love and seeing what only love can imagine. Love enables us to see what is beyond the moment, beyond the surface. If this can be true of our love, how much more is it true of God's love.

God's justice is an embodiment of his loving wisdom, which is radically different from the apparent wisdom of the world. We grow in this wisdom through deeper knowledge of, reflection on and living out God's written Word. Our growth in Scripture by the Spirit extends, deepens and strengthens our roots in God. Too many of us read the Bible the way we do everything else: for our own sakes. But living in the new environment of God's life asks more of us, namely that we do things out of love and concern for others.

I once participated in a small group that wanted to read the Bible for the sake of other people. We made a list of people whose circumstances were very different from our own: a lifer in prison, a single mom on welfare, a blind man, a mom with AIDS, a teenage runaway living on the streets. We knew these people personally. Instead of studying Bible texts for ourselves, we deliberately tried to study the texts for them. We asked how the Scripture would speak to them, how it might confuse or help them, what resources it might give them. It was a Bible study for the sake of the prisoner, the widow, the orphan, the oppressed. It taught all of us how little we think beyond our own frames of reference. It humbled us to see how much the blinders of our own experience distorted our ability to imagine what true grace might look like to people whose lives are dramatically different from ours.

Our church in Berkeley holds a similar Bible study, but the particular people in need are actually present. Each Saturday evening we host a meal for the homeless, and afterward they are invited to stay for a Bible study. The men and women who lead this ministry step into the other-world of street life, and the result is more unpredictable and nonlinear than they could have imagined. The leaders are convinced that by God's Spirit, the Bible speaks to everyone, even in the midst of broken, drug-infested, confused, angry, vulnerable lives. And they are right. It takes spiritual imagination to lead this group. These leaders challenge and inspire me to exercise the same gifts.[1]

When our reading of Scripture starts with remembering our new life in God, we begin to notice things that didn't appear noteworthy or relevant before. I've typically been a part of small-group Bible studies in which the members have a "majority culture" mindset. We read the Bible simply looking for some encouragement to go on about our lives, with all the security and prerogatives we already have, and add a little Jesus on top. So the parable of the good Samaritan was about how to be a good Samaritan rather than how to recognize and enter into the suffering of the one who was left by the side of the road. We identify with the one who offers help rather than understanding that we are the ones in need. This shows the poverty of our selfish imagination. Only because of the scandalous and unlikely heart of God in Christ, who "though he was rich, yet for [our] sakes he became poor" (2 Corinthians 8:9), have we who were lost been found. It's out of that life in God, both as the broken and the redeemed, that we look on others who are broken with hearts of God's compassion and mercy.

History gives us only a spotty view of the success rate of such other-centered Bible reading. Slavery was defended by many who knew Scripture backwards and forward—but their imaginations were unchanged. This process is clearly not automatic, and it ought to keep all of us humbled. Much of the time, we show where we live by how we read Scripture. We are meant to show where we live because of whose Word we read and actually obey. This is behind the remarkable message in the book of James, where the point is made repeatedly that if we truly believe, we will obey. Emphasizing the need for such consistency, James says that reading the Word and failing to obey is like someone who looks in the mirror, then steps away and immediately forgets what they look like (James 1:23-24). We are to be those who read and obey, who remember who we are and therefore where we live.

An Unexpected Family

Another resource for stimulating our imagination for justice is the body of Christ. One of the most wonderful and challenging parts of our new environment in the heart of God is the discovery that we are not alone! "We" are here: the church. For some this sounds like good news, and for others it sounds like something to squelch a God-breathed imagination.

Before I go any further, let me say that by this point in my thirty-year discipleship, I have come to deeply love the people of God—mostly. But I am a skeptic by nature, so loving the church has not been easy or natural for me. I understand those who say that the church itself is one of the biggest road blocks to their coming to faith in Christ. Of course, this makes the fact that I am a pastor even more surprising. Few things could seem less likely. I consider it an act of God's surprising imagination, not mine! I am grateful for this calling despite its unlikelihood. It's not necessarily the address I would have chosen. But all of God's people now dwell with many whom we would not have chosen. So here too we need to gain a view of God's greater imagination.

John Calvin said that the church is like a school, a place to learn and to test what is being learned. The community of God's people is like a test kitchen or a laboratory for the remaking of humanity in the likeness of Jesus Christ. Precisely because this is such an unexpected family, with people of every tribe and tongue and nation, with every personality and persuasion, it is a community where the issues of the entire human community at large can be faced and potentially applied. God's family, adopted by the sacrifice of Christ, includes Jew and Gentile alike. What we have in common is that we are all created in God's image, that we all fail to live like it and that by the grace of Father, Son and Spirit, we are invited into God's holy triune communion to regain our communion with God, with one another and with the world.

This will involve transformation in two ways. First and foremost we are called into this unexpected family to become more like one another in our character, since we are each called to be conformed to the character of God in Christ. At the same time, we are called into this unexpected family to become more distinct from one another in our created uniqueness, allowing the particular glory of God in us to be seen and fulfilled. These two callings require one another and will test one another. Both come from God's imagination.

My close friendships with people who are not like me are some of the greatest gifts God has given me. For example, Zac is a special brother in Christ who grew up in an African village in southern Uganda. He was raised in a strongly Christian family and also shaped by his tribal identity. As I got to know him, I realized that his cultural and spiritual starting points were not at all like mine. The history that has shaped his life, his tribe, his country and his continent are dramatically different from mine. But our paths crossed and we became friends. Zac's leadership, intellect, vision and above all his love for Jesus Christ mean that though I can't share his background or culture, there are few people I would rather resemble in character, heart and passion than Zac. No one would ever confuse us by looking from the outside, but by God's grace we will become more like each other from the inside.

Living-Giving Conformity

We can only grow in character, sharing the love, justice and mercy of God, as we grow together as God's people. Scripture sees justice as the practice of the community, not just the individual. Justice is about people in relationships, therefore seeking justice must be the work of people in relationship with each other. For us to carry the justice and mercy of God to others, we must learn from each other and with each other. I know that to the degree I have begun to learn and do mercy and justice in the world, to bear the signs of God's character being formed in me, it is due in large part to the people of God who have shown me what this looks like. Early in my Christian life I became aware of the remarkable power of mentors.

Other Christians, whether they were older or my peers or sometimes much younger, have been some of God's most powerful teachers in my life. Rob befriended me like few other people ever have. For about a decade it seemed that every important new opportunity for Christian growth was in some way a result of Rob's encouragement or challenge. Rob's heart for the world rubbed off on me. Brian gave me the example of a fine Christian leader. He was far more mature in life and faith, and he could be assertive as well as thoughtful and gentle. Tom showed me what zeal and spiritual fire look like, how easily it can come and go and how grace rescues us, even from ourselves sometimes. His ability and joy to move crossculturally was something I envied and learned from as well. Tom showed me that outrageous discipleship is not an oxymoron. Jane showed me the heart of a prayerful servant. She was already a mature disciple before I was born, and knowing her taught me that the long road of following Jesus Christ bears fruit that can be felt and seen. Tim helped me see how much friendship matters and how questions can open doors to relationships and faith. Steve showed me the place of encouragement, risk and hope. These are just some of the models God gave me to change me and help me grow.

Seeing myself in entirely new ways through the eyes of these and other mentors over the years has altered how I live. I have also seen negative examples in the body of Christ. Some "brothers" and "sisters" have hurt the work of grace in my life or in lives of others, or have done despicable things in the name of the God we both claim to worship and serve. Indeed, the history of God's people in Scripture and beyond provides damning testimony of the character and actions of some who have affirmed the faith. The poverty of imagination in the body of Christ causes many to continue suffering in the world. That poverty is not just in others, but also in me.

The aspect of the "problem of evil" that I struggle with most is not the generalized suffering of the innocent, as big as that issue is. Rather, for me it is this conundrum: if God is all-powerful and all-good, why are God's people so unchanged? This issue is worthy of far longer treatment than I can give it here, but I mention it to express the seriousness and difficulty of the church being God's agent of justice and mercy in the world when we show need of such transformation ourselves.

Perhaps that is the point. God's work of re-creating all things, especially the church, is a necessary and difficult work. It's beyond my imagination. Scripture tells us that God in Christ has done on the cross what is the most decisive action necessary to secure that transformation. However, it is a work that goes on in God's people—and we see just how virulent, resistant and free we are in rejecting God's work in our lives. If this is true among those in whom Christ dwells by the power of the Holy Spirit and who now dwell in Christ in God, then let's abandon any naivete about what it will take to live and do the work of justice in the world.

We are not called to be idealists about the church. That's fantasy, not sanctified imagination. That's a false, distorted, immature imagination. Instead we are to practice hope for the church. We cannot say, "Look at Christ, not the church," when Jesus says, "I want people to look at you and see me." The family of God's people is neither a utopian society nor a negligible witness. Again, this is what makes the church a school living within the heart of God: a place to vigorously, profoundly and slowly grow into the likeness of Jesus as we seek (and don't seek) God, as we love (and don't love) each other, as we do (and don't do) justice in the world. God is in the mess that is the church, and the mess that is the church is in God.

Liberating Variation

The other aspect of our transformation expresses God's wonderful creativity in creating a people of such diversity. As we become more like one another in character (because we are being conformed to Jesus Christ), we are liberated to become more distinct (because we are God's unique creation). It is evil and its derivatives, not goodness, that fundamentally yield a world of sameness. Homogeneity is not apparent in the natural world of God's mind-boggling imagination. Socialization, whether mainstream or radical, makes sameness a sign of belonging. In forms of dress, music, speech, attitude and actions, much socialization offers a framework that denies our uniqueness and suppresses God's distinct intentions for each of us.

Society in general does this. Globalization now makes it possible for this sameness to be bred around the world. It is a tragic loss of God's imaginative creation in each of us. "Everybody's doing it" is a signal that something wonderful is being lost. We are meant to be conformed in character but endlessly varied in the creativity of how that character gets embodied and enacted in each of our lives, bodies, personalities and settings. This becomes lost in a world where we are so unacceptable to ourselves, where we do almost anything to show we belong, where we are painfully bound by a self-consciousness that restricts us from being fully and distinctly ourselves. We sell ourselves to Faustian idols of acceptance, popularity, invisibility and success.

Sadly, this is just as true among God's people as anywhere else. We show once again that we have forgotten where we live and that safe worship does not transform our imaginations. In the boundlessness of God's love, we are meant to find the freedom to live our creatureliness in safety, confidence and liberation. The church is meant to help each other do that. Part of our role of loving one another, of building each other up in love, is to set one another free for this kind of life.

But so often we don't. We panic and live like the surrounding society, forgetting that what we have been offered is so much more than what "everybody's doing." We are meant to find in our communion with God and enact in our communion with one another the ability to truly see and love the individual and the community, to seek the welfare of the one and the many.

Part of our capacity to lean into the work of justice as worship comes from the celebration and the joy of God's unique act of creativity that has fashioned every life. In the church, learning and discovering this should give us a passion for the full work of grace in those not yet in the community of faith. Our growing capacity to see the one in the midst of the many is meant to shatter the categories under which people suffer: "the poor," "the lame," "the prisoners," "the lost." The Good Shepherd values the many and the one. That same Good Shepherd wants us to learn and enact that same set of values. We are meant to imagine things God's way, and that includes imagining our uniqueness alongside our conformity before God.

A Deeper Love

Economists argue that all relationships are economic. That is, every relationship has a cost-benefit aspect. We may or may not like to calibrate relationships to be equitable. Indeed, some clearly don't want that but prefer instead to be in debt, or that others be in debt to them. Whatever the case, we can't find a human space where relationships are not shaped by this kind of economics.

To the degree that common sense and experience allow us to be honest, economists are describing something we may find distasteful but would have a difficult time denying. One of the assumptions of the economic model of relationships is that we all have need and that scarcity is an ever-present reality.

God's loving imagination operates on different terms. Growth in Christian discipleship, moving toward maturity in Christ, shifts these terms considerably. Again, if we remember where we live, in the unmerited grace of God whose love can never be bargained for nor ever run out, we have a very different starting point for love. Agape love is not natural to us, but it is natural to the God in whom we now live and whose love is meant to fill and satisfy us. That's God's imagination. Paul knew this and prayed that the Ephesians would come to know the "breadth and length and height and depth" of the love of God (Ephesians 3:18). As we live in the One who is love and as we seek to practice that love toward those in God's family, we come to relationships freed from the economic realities of cost, benefit and scarcity.

I met a woman named Katherine in a night commuter camp in northern Uganda. She was a volunteer who came every night just to be a caring adult presence in the camp. I asked her how she came to be involved in this effort. She explained that she lived nearby and that her husband could stay with their own children at night so she could be with these children. She had been doing this every night for several years. When I pressed her for her motivation, she said with the plainest conviction, "I go again and again to Holy Communion, and I know how much God loves me. How can I not come here?" Worship drew her to tangible, costly love.

Giving love away can seem scary to us. If we love, our world of scarcity says we may lose. No imagination there. So we better love those who will love us back, who show the means to do that. This often leads to the false and distorted conclusion that loving those who suffer, who face injustice, who are in pain or some kind of need means we will be the losers, and we simply can't run that risk. In the vulnerable place many of us live, this cultural pattern seems plainly evident.

A few years ago I was in a serious bicycle accident on a remote path near the East Bay of San Francisco. It was a scary experience. Though no one else was injured, it was a messy scene with a lot of blood, and at first no one was willing to help me. Several people came along the path, but they were afraid of blood contact. Eventually I got the help I needed, and my injuries from that accident are now healed. But those moments on the bike path serve as a reminder to me of the anxiety we have these days over loving our neighbor. Serving is messy. It could be infectious. If I were to love, I might lose. God's imagination of love includes all possibilities.

Giving Love Away

The gospel of Jesus first nourishes us with a kind of love that comes freely (no cost-benefit) and without limit (no scarcity). We need to practice living in that love and living off of that love. How do we do this? By risking giving it away. If we wait till we think we have hoarded enough love in the "love bank," it will be like the manna, which could not be saved and even began to rot. Instead we grow in experiencing God's free, unlimited love by giving it away.

A Christian small group, a prayer partner, a spiritual director or a good Christian friend can be of enormous help here. We can grow through the help and accountability of others who can help us love beyond our comfort zone, beyond the point of easy reciprocity from those who will love us back. Some of us may have been wounded enough in the past that we need special caution and patience in taking these steps. However, there is no other way to grow in our own experience of God's love and in our ability to love in God's name.

A wonderful man I know was out of town when he discovered that his wife had been having an affair. This was not the first time it had happened, and the news was beyond devastating to him. The first call he made after learning the news was to his mens' small group, asking them to pray. He gave them the basic details of the story, but he knew that in his brokenness he needed his brothers in Christ to be there for him. So the first thing he did the night after he returned home was meet with this group of brothers to weep and pray. He has told me several times that he doesn't know how he could have continued in his life and work and pursuing the healing of his marriage were it not for the openhearted love of this small group of guys. They helped him imagine a future he could not see on his own.

Is there someone you know who is in need, whom you can regularly seek to love with as few strings as possible? The discipline of prayer, as we have discussed, can be the first step in doing so. But take other steps as well. Seek to love freely, without expectations of something in return, without the assumption that it is ever going to be relevant. Pray for wisdom and sensitivity to love in a way that the other person(s) can receive as love, whether they acknowledge it as such or not. Praise and thank God for making them the unique creation they are. Think of how you might love them in ways that set them free to be their unique selves.

When Rosa Parks chose not to move from her seat on the bus, she was trusting God's imagination for goodness and justice. She might not have said it that way, of course. She was simply trying to get home. But her assumption about how and why that should be done was simply not in the imaginations of the other passengers or of many other people in her daily life. She was right in her vision. She saw and loved what others could not see and embrace. She loved a just reality as it was meant to be, and she gave herself away toward that end. It was an unexpected and transformative act of love.

A Wider Communion

An important part of our imagination for justice comes from realizing that our life in God has placed us in a much wider communion with others. If our address is in the life of God, and the world is in the heart of God, then the address where we live is immeasurably wider than just "our people."

I had the joy and privilege of being raised in a fairly large extended family. Since my maternal grandmother was the matriarch of her eight siblings and their families, and since she lived with us, our home became the gathering place for the family. These were joyful, wonderful caring people for whom I am very grateful. I learned that these were "my people."

It took the gospel and slowly growing into maturity for me to discover that God had a heart that was wide enough to include those who were clearly not "my people." I have to admit that reading the Gospel accounts of Jesus' ministry was not comfortable for me. "My people" included my family and other people I chose. *My* was clearly the operative term.

Then I met Jesus Christ. The first shock was that his heart was big enough to include me and "my people." The more I reflected on that, the greater I realized God's love to be. I could see it was a love that would send me and others who are Christ's to live out the wider, more varied, more problematic communion that is God's great heart for the world. I could see this was the plan, but I was not at ease with what it meant.

To start with, it meant I would see that God's love included other Christian people I had previously discounted, judged and disregarded and still struggled with. It meant that the awkward, ignorant-sounding, closed-minded Christian nerd I had known growing up was now my brother in Christ! This was new territory for me. It meant that the social ladder I had used needed to be thrown away. This was both terrifying and exhilarating to me. I was both shocked and relieved by this call. It meant that my new life in God was going to ask a lot more of me than I found easy or even desirable. Still, I could sense that it was right and true. I deliberately tried to connect with this former schoolmate, to practice stretching my heart. What I discovered was a remarkable person. He was more mature in his faith than I was, and his sense of compassion and joy pointed me to a far wider world than I had expected. My imagination was changing.

I have taken many other steps over the years, with those both near and far from me. Sometimes it has meant affirming that others are included in God's communion, sometimes reaffirming that I see them that way. Often it has involved growth and change, and frequently it has meant some kind of dying to myself or to my expectations. It has meant discovering again and again how much joy there is in entering into God's global communion and trying to love God's way.

When I read Isaiah and Jeremiah, the people who seem to be most on God's heart are those who suffer most: the blind, the poor, the widow, the orphan. That's still not as instinctively apparent in my daily life as I wish it would be, but it is becoming far more evident than it used to be. As I become freer from anxiety about the economics of love and the fears of scarcity, the Holy Spirit has gradually helped me learn to love with a greater heart.

God has often and quite distinctly used people with severe cerebral palsy to enlarge my heart. The most recent of these teachers is Dustin Webb. When Dustin was born, his parents were told to just institutionalize him since he would have no capacities, even for relationship. This turned out to be far from the case, and the love of his parents and sisters has made all the difference in his life, just as they would say Dustin's love has made all the difference in theirs. Technology has now made it possible for others to know the richness of Dustin's perspective and reflections, as well as his humor and his love of baseball. I have meditated frequently on his writings, which are distinct and profound. During the years that Dustin and his family attended our church's worship services,

Dustin would sometimes groan with "sighs too deep for words," you might say. It would occur without warning and quite audibly. It seemed to me it often happened in moments of silence or at a pause in the service. I always received this sound as a great gift, one of the most honest offerings given in those services, and I wanted to link all of our groans to Dustin's. Higher praise to God would be hard to imagine.

God has also given me other mentors in compassion whose simple daily acts have shown me that even though I can't do everything, I can still do something to love those in need. My travels to parts of Africa and Asia have been deliberate investments in asking God to extend and enlarge my grasp of the compassion and commitment of God to people facing injustice and need. These have restocked my imagination with the faces, the tastes, smells and tears of injustice.

A friend of mine was in Rwanda recently and met a woman who had lost forty-one members of her family, including all of her own children, in the genocide. She had contracted HIV/AIDS from the multiple rapes she had suffered. As she began to emerge from the shock and horror of all that had happened, she returned to her village to find many orphans who needed care. Since then she has taken on raising two young boys, one of whom is also HIV positive. They are a new family. She realized that some of the people in her village were among those who had killed her family and raped her. She faced a decision: she could live the rest of her life in bitterness, or she could forgive and seek to serve even those perpetrators around her. Because of God's grace, she has chosen to do the latter. So in the very context where her family was killed and she herself was raped, contracted HIV/AIDS and will die, she and her new sons are now seeking to love their neighbors.

When Jesus says we gain our life by losing it, he speaks of this remarkable communion in which we are invited to have a stake. I now live in the Bay Area, but Kitgum, Uganda, and Gitarama, Rwanda, and Calcutta, India, are part of my address. People in need in such places, who suffer as the poor and the widow and the orphan, are now "my people." I now know that because I live in Christ in God, if these who are "my people" suffer, then faithful worship will call me into sharing in their suffering and seeking justice on their behalf. That's because I am learning where I live and the difference it makes. I am starting to imagine with the heart of God.[2]

A Wiser Humility

J. B. Phillips's translation of Romans 12:3 has always appealed to me: "Have a sane estimate of your capabilities." In a biblical context, such sanity requires us to see ourselves in relation to our Creator, to our fellow human beings and to the whole created order. Faithful worship is one of the best gifts in the face of our greatest arrogance (we can do anything) or in the face of our greatest self-negation (we can do nothing). When the psalmist despaired over the observation that the unrighteous flourish while the righteous suffer, it was too much for him to ponder "until I went into the sanctuary of God; / then I perceived their end" (Psalm 73:17). In other words, worship brought clarity and trust by showing what was in God's imagination.

On the other end of the spectrum, worship sometimes does its best work by upsetting our clarity and trust in various things: unmasking our smugness, our selfishness, our arrogance and our independence from God. Peter learned this while fishing. After an exhausting night, Jesus said to put out again from the shore and let down the nets. Peter protests but obeys. When the nets break because of the load of fish, Peter rushes to bow at Jesus' feet and confesses, "Go away from me, Lord, for I am a sinful man!" (Luke 5:8).

A life in Christ in God, a life of worship, will lead us to make one of the most important of life's discoveries: we are not the center of it all! Life is not, finally, about us. It is not only possible, but it is far healthier and more meaningful to live a life that is about far more than the satisfaction of our desires, the meeting of our needs, the entertainment of our bodies and imaginations. This kind of liberated humility emerges out of a deep sense of our worth, not our worthlessness. It comes out of a correspondingly greater concern for the worth of the others we seek to serve in the name of their Maker and ours, their Redeemer and ours, their Comforter and ours.

The body of Christ is meant to practice living with the humility and imagination that demonstrates we know "that [we] belong, body and soul, in life and in death, not to [our]self but to [our] faithful savior Jesus Christ."[3] This does not mean you have to start by resigning your job and moving to Mozambique. It genuinely starts by the practices of prayer and reading and praying through Scripture seeking more than just our own blessing. It starts by asking God to enlarge our heart, give us eyes to see people in need in our immediate community and gradually see people beyond that too. To do this faithfully is to practice living our life in God. It changes everything.

The next steps toward practicing wiser humility as an expression of our new address require the offering of some of our time. Imagine this is why, in fact, God has given you the time you have. This must come from the conviction that your time (like all the rest of your life) belongs to God for his purposes. And what are God's purposes? To live a life of righteousness and justice. Humility offers time, and then it offers thought and effort and talent. It eventually means offering ourselves, in all our fears and anxieties, plans and skills. After all, it's the whole of us that lives where we do, and it's the whole of us that's created and needed to show such love and justice to others.

But It Will Stink!

In the story of the death of Lazarus, Lazarus' sisters Mary and Martha are clearly distressed that Jesus did not come sooner to heal his friend. Yet after Jesus' arrival and heartfelt tears, when he asks that the stone covering Lazarus' tomb be rolled away, they protest: "Lord, already there is a stench because he has been dead four days" (John 11:39). It will stink. Jesus responds by asking, "Did I not tell you that if you believed, you would see the glory of God?"(v. 40).

Over and over again we are stopped by the repulsion of the stink, even when Jesus is offering God's glory. To live lives of faithful worship, to cultivate God's imagination for justice, to trust Jesus Christ to do a work of liberation and transformation means there will be times when our noses will be filled with the stench of human need and evil. But far more profoundly, we will also have glimpses of the glory of God that can set the captives free. That is God's imagination.

"I have a dream," Martin Luther King Jr. proclaimed. Do we?

10

Living Awake

IF WE WANT TO LIVE AWAKE TO GOD AND GOD'S PURPOSES IN THE world, where do we start and then how do we continue? It must involve at least four things.

Choosing to Live Our Worship

No one can worship for us. We have to decide for ourselves to worship faithfully and fully. We have to open our hearts and minds to reality, specifically to the reality of God in Jesus Christ. Then we choose to actually live it out every day, in the most ordinary and extraordinary circumstances.

This means living a vision of life in which we are not at the center. God is. It means turning away from a vision in which we and our issues are the primary focus of the day. God is. In a life of faithful worship, our life is not about us. It's about God.

This kind of radical awakening does not occur overnight. It takes time. It is the work of our whole life and is only fully accomplished in eternity. It's the gradual unveiling of what is true, so we are not equipped to move there in just one step. We will move ahead and then back, again and again. It doesn't mean that we give up our preferences, personalities or choices. What is gradually altered is the controlling urgency, the unequivocal and unquestioned preeminence these things have over us. By the power of the Holy Spirit, we choose to live each day leaning into our new life in Christ and practicing this way of being and doing. Such a life is the fruit of the Holy Spirit.

Central to this process is communion not only with the Father, Son and Spirit but also with the community of God's people, the church. When others in the body of Christ are our teachers and partners in these matters, the process of waking up can unfold in larger strides. For me, friendships with those who live and serve in contexts of threat or danger, violence or suffering, have been extremely important. To know those who live in Christ for the sake of others while facing overwhelming circumstances all around them has been transformative for me. I have already told the stories of some of these people.

Knowing these friends who risk their lives every time they proclaim the gospel means I look differently at the risks in my life. Because of the courage of a friend in Southeast Asia who takes it for granted that he will probably be imprisoned again in the future simply for being a Christian leader, I look differently at the lesser dangers I face. I do not have the same daily circumstances, but knowing something of the reality faced by this brother in Christ means that I come to corporate worship, personal prayer and public life with more of God's heart and power than I might do otherwise. I seldom worship without thinking of friends in places around the globe who face similar challenges. Knowing that we are in one new community together changes how I live, which changes how my family lives and how our congregation lives.

I have seen that those who practice finding their security in Christ live differently from those who find their security in alarms or money or withdrawal. They walk in freedom wherever they are. They are not naive to the realities of danger, but they are not controlled by such circumstances. We call people who know the language of the street and all its subtle implications *streetwise*. The people I am talking about are *God-wise* because they walk in the streets, serve in places of danger, know the experience of suffering, and do so with freedom and joy. My friend in Malaysia is no fool, but he walks in spiritual freedom because he knows his life is not his own, but God's. He is awake to God in the midst of darkness. Knowing such people awakens me.

It's not that I live vicariously through the example of these friends. It's that their example calls me to greater risks and courage where I live. I remember the day it dawned on me as a young disciple that since I belong to Christ, I belong to the church and the church belongs to me. I remember the vulnerability I felt as a new believer attending college in a skeptical, secular environment. There were people around me that I wanted to love but found intimidating or overpowering. It struck me that this was not a calling I had to shoulder alone. God's idea was that this was the work of the community of God's people. Loving those around me was something I could do with others. This also changed my ability to respond to less dramatic challenges.

I needed the Christian community around me, not just for my sake but for the sake of my neighbor as well. The community would help me, and as it did I believed it would help me love others. Often that's exactly what happened. Not always, of course, but that too is a part of the ongoing challenge of living our lives as Christ's disciples. It was during that time I began to realize how much the public witness of God's people rises or falls on whether we actually live out our identity.

Living out our identity in Christ, oddly enough, involves small acts of dying, of losing our life in order to find it (Luke 9:24). We must die to the things that keep us asleep. This means stepping into a Philippians 2 way of life: "Let the same mind be in you that was in Christ Jesus, who, though he was in the form of God, did not regard equality with God as something to be exploited, but emptied himself, taking the form of a slave. . . . he humbled himself and became obedient to the point of death—even death on a cross" (Philippians 2:5-8).

We have to practice laying aside our unflappable pursuit of our own satisfaction, entertainment, pleasure or routine in order to pursue God and ask him to reorder our priorities and passions. We have to cultivate dying to the overpowering appetites that our culture hyperstimulates daily in order to become increasingly stimulated by God's grace and imagination and to desire that what is on God's heart be on ours.

Sabbath-keeping practiced can unhook us from appetite-driven and production-driven machine of our culture. It helps us discover the liberty of saying no in order to say yes. Identification with God's rest on a weekly basis can foster some of the spiritual and emotional resources we need to see and feel beyond ourselves. What a priority-calibrating gift it is to take a full day every week to rest and realign your life with the passions of God! No to busyness. No to unnecessary consumption. No to 24-7 productivity. No to media. Yes to God. Yes to worship. Yes to community. Yes to justice.

Daily spiritual disciplines also add a significant part in deepening the process of practicing our true identity. Prayer and Bible study are tools God uses to transform us by the renewal of our minds. This means not just reading the Scriptures but pursuing the heart of God in the Scriptures. If our discipleship is mostly shaped by certain overly familiar parts of the Bible, perhaps it is time to meditate on other parts of "the whole counsel of God" (Acts 20:27 NKJV) Our biblical and theological vision is meant to enhance our sight. Central to Christians' lives is a growing vision of God that Scripture gives us. We are not merely to look at Scripture (reading it) but to look through Scripture (seeing with it). This means, of course, we must grow in our knowledge of Scripture in order to put on such lenses.

For example, in relation to issues of worship and justice, you might spend the next year focusing on a study of Isaiah or Jeremiah or Amos. You might use some study guides to help you get your bearing on the text. Primarily, however, try asking God to give you insight into his heart as revealed through these prophets, and to help you grow in mirroring that heart. Do you understand the passions of God in these texts? Do those burdens trouble you as well? If you do this and then enact the passion of God toward the lost, the forgotten, the needy and the poor, you will find by grace that worship and justice are of one piece. And your life will be far more awake.

Pastoral leadership is key to helping a church step toward the real dangers of worship. Pastors need to honestly and publicly grapple with these dimensions of their biblical call and how to work it out with their congregation. Church leaders needs to be engaged. This is not a call to politicize the pulpit or the church's ministry. It is a call to hear again the words of Scripture about our public discipleship and to let such words continue to renew our vision of God and our actions in the world. As we discussed earlier, our worship needs to speak to issues of power.

Each summer I propose a year-long preaching plan in the context of a five-year vision of the biblical material that we will seek to study together. Some churches benefit from lectionary preaching, but our tradition is to do series of expository sermons through various books or sections of the Bible, with some topical series as well. I seek to work regularly with both Old and New Testament texts. We need the whole counsel of God to feed a comprehensive vision of our discipleship, both personal and public.

My goal is to preach the text and let it make its own application. I try not to preach ideologically or prescriptively. I don't take or advocate particular political positions in my sermons because I would be guilty of making it a bully pulpit and also because I respect the thoughtfulness and diversity of our congregation too much. Instead I try to provide other opportunities for congregational discussion of issues and implications of my sermons. It is more appropriate for me to express my own political views in that separate setting, where give-and-take is possible.

In our church, worship planning is done by the pastors and music leaders. We try to incorporate worship practices that encourage everyone to engage and participate. Our three Sunday services fall into categories from traditional to contemporary, but we work hard to keep such descriptions from becoming straitjackets. We want to honor core theological and liturgical values while remaining light on our feet and flexible about how those are carried out in any given service. We try to create worship practices that open doors for the Spirit of God to do whatever it chooses while our controls are present without dominating. We have certainly not arrived, but we are making progress.

The musical element of worship is profoundly important. The music that is available to draw from is less rich than we would wish in terms of justice themes. We have therefore become ever more diverse in some of our musical choices. We have also benefited greatly from the creativity of our staff and church members, using some of their own compositions that are built around sermon series or themes. Much of this has been experimental but has been well received and has given voice to some of the movements in worship we want to encourage.

We have found that physical movement in either style of service can be an important element in communicating that worship is a response and a set of actions. Worship practices that involve individual movement combined with times when the whole congregation acts at once can be valuable parts of affirming our faith by action. We then build on this by expressing how these same actions take us out into the world to live as disciples—in our offerings, in our service, in our touch, in our confessions or in our hope.

Wakeful and faithful worship encompasses the whole of life. It is not a discretionary activity. It is not a nod toward God out of religious duty, nor is it measured by sincerity. Before the benediction at the end of the service I often say something like this: "The measure of our worship is the fruit of character and action that looks more and more like the character and action of God. Let's live like those who have worshiped our Lord Jesus Christ."

Choosing to See

One of the realities of being human is living with limited vision. We are finite, and we are fallen. We don't see perfectly or comprehensively or fairly or truly. We see as the limited people we are. We also see in distorted ways as a sign of our own self-interest. This means we see selectively, prejudicially and unfairly. Human sight at its best is not very good. It is, however, sufficient for acts of love and justice offered in humility.

We can choose to become better seers. That may seem obvious, but it is a huge step. It means deciding to live with eyes wide open to God and to the purposes of God in the world. It also means living with eyes wanting to see what truly is, whether or not it is appealing, attractive, desirable or comfortable. We cultivate selective vision purposely because in our cultural and personal bias, we want to see some things and definitely do not want to see others. Truly seeing can be awkward and disruptive. In fact it should be so.

No seer is ever without prejudice. Everyone sees through a combination of lenses. Scripture is given specifically to help humanity see God and ourselves more clearly. If reality came into existence through the initiative of a loving and personal Creator, then seeing our world and our fellow human beings from God's point of view (which is the purpose of Scripture) means we can come to see the world differently and better.

Coming to see the poor, the forgotten, the imprisoned and so on may mean making the effort to look in places we don't normally see. Short-term mission trips can help give us new vision. When we go on such adventures, we should be prepared to see with every sense and to ask God to help us see with the heart and wisdom of Jesus. When I have had the privilege of going on such trips, I have earnestly prayed that God would use the experience to burn into the eyes of my heart the images of the people and needs and circumstances so I will not forget and will not see the same way as I did before.

On one such trip I stood on the broken veranda of a once-glorious Victorian mansion on the Hooghly River in Dhaka, Bangladesh. For years the mansion had been filled with poor squatters living in it. Prodip, a Bangladeshi friend of mine, stood with me on the veranda. As we faced the river, it took a few moments for my eyes to adjust to the smoky air at dusk and to begin to take in what was before me. We were looking at a vast pile of hovels, precariously pieced together in what had once been glorious gardens stretching to the river. Now the poorest of Dhaka's poor eked out a survival. Prodip himself was very poor. He had lived in Dhaka his whole life, but he had never taken a cycle rickshaw until that day because the fifty-cent ride was too costly for him. His circumstances were far better than what we saw before us. Prodip said, "People live here because they have not yet been able to die." I see the world differently because of Prodip's vision.

The key to short-term missions is that they are just that: short-term. Much can be said for these trips as exposure experiences for enhancing our sensitivity and awareness. Often the short-term impact is dramatic. There are many stories expressing the value of such trips. But we need to be aware of the danger of becoming missionary tourists who see and feel but do not follow through (whether here or there) in sustained ways that take seriously the need and call. Such a trip may make us feel more in touch, but our relative inaction doesn't show how it matters. A Rwandan HIV/AIDS nurse told me, "I often show people around this clinic. But I want to tell you, we don't need you to come and see all this need if you are going to go home and forget us. We need you to remember us and act on what you have seen."

This is why it is so important to spend as much time as possible with local Christians on such trips. Try to see and feel their world as much as you can. I try to live and act in the Bay Area in ways that reflect seeing with the eyes of those I know in India, Uganda, South Africa, Rwanda, Kenya, China, Bangladesh, Sri Lanka and Mexico.

Another way our vision can grow is by choosing to focus on some particular issue of injustice in the world that God has laid on our heart, then committing to keep it before us all the time. Internet news services can

be helpful by linking to relevant stories. Finding others to share this burden and pray with us is another great step. The point is to develop eyes
that see need and see God in relation to that need. As you do this, pray
for discernment in how you might respond. Whom could you write to?
Where might you give? What tangible action could you take to make a
difference? What ministries or organizations might help channel your
steps? Who could you ask to be part of it with you?

Seeing is not easy business. It demands a lot. It can be tiring and
sometimes unpleasant. It means carrying in our minds unresolved pain
and need. It means abandoning the enclave we might have been hiding
in. We won't be able to sleep quite as soundly. The things we thought
mattered we will now consider of little or no importance. It's not easy to
live as an exile—Jesus said we could depend on that. This is what drives
us back, to need to see God afresh, to need to grow in our capacity to
"let the same mind be in [us] that was in Christ Jesus" (Philippians 2:5).

Choosing to Engage

Hebrews 13:3 gives us a stunning admonition to engagement: "Remember those who are in prison, as though you were in prison with
them; those who are being tortured, as though you yourselves were being tortured." This injunction is characteristic of the gospel. It expresses what true empathy means. To live it out, however, means practicing our exilic life and leaning into foreign territory—the
circumstances of someone else. That's the basic premise of our incarnational calling. It's about entering, engaging, acting on behalf of
someone else's reality as though it were our own. In Christ it is our
own. That's the depth of our biblical call to justice.

Having an attitude of caring, while important, is not the same as demonstrating compassion. Being able to recognize need is also key. But it is
not the same as doing something. This book is not just about awakening
our conscience and our heart. It is about the role worship is meant to

have in awakening us so we actually live differently. It is a call to worship that *does* justice.

What counts as engagement? It involves our time, talent, money, effort, imagination, freedom and prerogatives. Engagement moves beyond merely having compassion and gathering information to demonstrable action. Here the decisions of living an awakened life will be ones that move us into relationship, into participation that is the privilege and the price of doing justice. We need to take steps that are personal and particular, and we need to take steps that are corporate and systemic. Those in the body of Christ have to demonstrate both levels of action. If we are prone to accept a person-centered response to issues of injustice instead of a system-centered approach, we are not taking seriously enough what it means to affirm "Jesus is Lord." Action is needed at both levels, and different parts of the body of Christ are needed to express each.

On the personal level, you might start with a careful inventory of the circumstances of people already in your life. Perhaps there is someone who has already given you information about their own needs to which you could respond. The first place to look may be to a nearby neighbor or colleague or friend.

Or you might begin with a phone call to your church or a local agency to find out how you could help people in your town. This might mean driving to a meeting. It could involve signing up to be responsible for something. It might mean going back every week and doing the same thing. Or it might involve a season of specially concentrated energy or commitment. And then you might take the next step deeper as a result.

We are not called to manic action. We are to practice lives of sustained, sacrificial service. We have to focus and stay on task. We need to approach our engagement realizing that justice is not a seasonal need. Where is God calling us (individually or collectively) to a protracted period of dedicated self-giving? Finding out requires a persistent willingness to live a life that puts the needs of the forgotten, the neglected and the needy higher on our daily priority list.

It also involves practicing moving into places and toward people in need. This is a challenge, especially for most middle-class white people. I should know—I'm one of them. Our subculture is gripped with fear about real need. It is about *not* being in vulnerable places. Yet the work of the kingdom, the purpose of God, is specifically to go to places or people in need. If white middle-class culture distinguishes itself from others in the pecking order of culture, we face a significant hurdle in crossing over or moving beyond that demarcation. It's about learning to live with a wise openness toward others, finding ways of being available and alert and responsive.

This is just how doing justice unfolded for Randy Roth. He is a pastor in the Evangelical Covenant denomination who has served faithfully and well. His church was located in the Oakland hills and served a diverse group of people. He became more and more aware of the needs in the Oakland schools. Among its many other crises, the school district had been in state receivership for several years. Randy came to feel God's call to seek the *shalom* of the city, specifically to respond to the needs of all the kids falling behind in their academic lives. In time Randy took the bold step of leaving his secure position as a pastor to launch Faith Network, a ministry that provides volunteer tutors in needy schools. What started as a small grass-roots effort has steadily grown, winning the trust and support of the large and diverse Oakland School District. Randy's courage and faithfulness has in turn led people from our congregation and many others to find their place making a real difference in students' lives. From this shared trust came the opportunity for us to partner with Faith Network in launching the same kind of effort in Berkeley schools.

On the individual level, our actions do not have to be heroic. Even though we cannot do everything, it doesn't mean we can't do anything. Instead we need to be instructed by a simpler and more pervasive call. As Mother Teresa put it, "We cannot do great things in this world, we can only do little things with great love."[1] Or put another way, Pascal said, "Do small things as if they were great, because of the majesty of Jesus Christ. Do great things as if they were small and easy, because of his almighty power."[2]

Every day many people in my congregation pass by people living on the streets in Berkeley or San Francisco. Some are called to help respond to the macroproblem of homelessness. But any of us can learn the names of one or two homeless people and engage in ways beyond the surface "spare a quarter" requests. Others respond by serving at our Saturday night meals for the homeless or leading the Bible study after the meal. These are not heroic acts, but they imitate Christ.

I was moved several years ago when some of our college students, many of whom come from suburban contexts, began a ministry of foot washing at the drop-in medical clinic our church hosts. The students decided that while they didn't have medical skills or much money to help those who panhandle in our neighborhood every day, they could wash the feet of the homeless. This is an amazing gift for people whose feet are often in terrible condition. A simple touch is infrequent for many on the street, but here is a ministry of compassionate engagement that is sacrificial, earnest, personal, free and surprising. It sounds like the gospel because it is.

Action is also needed on the systemic level. Though this is fraught with more potential for both politics and contention, within the church and outside of it, we need not become paralyzed by those complications. If a congregation is inexperienced, it may be best to start by simply encouraging individual members to give of their time and expertise in responding to a given need. For example, I have had many conversations recently with individuals in our church who are seeking to respond to the immigration crisis we face as a nation. We have not taken collective action as a congregation, and we have been praying for and supporting individuals who are trying to seek justice for immigrants.

Some congregations a strong tradition of entering the political process and local, regional, state or national debates. This is not true of my congregation in Berkeley. We agree that given the broad political diversity of our congregation, it would be difficult and unlikely to find consensus in a congregational vote to take coordinated action. We therefore try to grow in our capacity to discuss and debate such things as a congregation, and encourage individuals to take steps as they see fit to address systemic change. Some have pursued elected office, some have sought appointments in various settings to attempt change, some have become more active letter writers. This latter step is one I have adopted, writing more frequently in recent years to elected representatives, expressing my opinion over various state or national issues and encouraging policies and actions that are supportive of justice concerns.

To sustain these personal and systemic efforts points again to the place of community. Individual and corporate worship that affirms and remembers, seeks and prays for such engagement is vital. We easily forget why we are doing these things. We find the sustained challenges draining, and we need renewal and encouragement. We mistakenly give in to voices that call us back to sleep rather than heeding those that call us to stay awake by living in God's rest. Liturgies can exercise and affirm our new grammar, and help us practice saying together what we may only hear when we are gathered with God's people. We need to sing out the truth and hope to which we are committed, and we need to be bound to a community that seeks God's mercy and justice with us, sometimes in the face of staggering opposition and human impossibility. We need to be with people who are trying to say no to the wrong things and yes to the right ones. We need to do so again and again.

Choosing to Love

Of all the mysteries of God's plans and purposes, none is more remarkable to me than his radical commitment to our freedom. In the midst of all we do that is counter to God's will, God does not strip us of the burden and challenge of freedom itself. Why? Because freedom is central to love. And that means it is central to why and how we are created to live.

Love has been so sentimentalized in our culture that putting love and justice into the same sentence sounds as dissonant as joining worship and justice. Yet all these things are intertwined in the character of God, none separable from the others. They are qualities intrinsic to God's being, and each one names God's life in different ways. None is to be present without the other.

When we live awake in the name of Jesus Christ, we choose to love openhandedly and openheartedly. When we choose to love in the name of Christ for the sake of justice, we allow our compassion to take us to people and to places for the sake of the other person, in advocacy for their need, out of a compassion for their suffering, even when it means sacrifice and suffering for us. This is not sentimentality; it is Christlike love.

Vigorously honest worship, whether personal or corporate, is meant to be the primary love feast in our lives. It's meant to be the context where we experience being known and loved as we are. It's meant to be the setting where we affirm our home in God's heart, seeing, tasting, hearing and sharing the love of Christ with one another. Out of this greenhouse of grace, we move back into a world in need of that love to which our lives are meant to bear witness.

When our worship pursues safety, the church becomes tempted to cocoon itself from the world, seeking and fostering an environment of security and safety that keeps in what we judge to be desirable and keeps out the undesirable. In a broken world full of dangers and injustices, this instinct can be as basic as personal self-preservation or as elaborate as a gated community. Love is preserved for those inside our cocoon. Within that boundary, love may be challenging but it is at least clearly defined and expected to be mutually given and received.

Meanwhile, injustice daily rips into and ruins the cocoons of others. Everyone longs for legitimate safety from power abuse, for a cocoon of protection to survive and thrive. In a world of injustice, where cocoon building and protection is often a personal and cultural obsession, it can be overwhelmingly scary to put your cocoon at risk by loving someone whose cocoon has been ripped or destroyed. We are culturally and psychologically terrified to get that close. Our love doesn't easily reach that far or risk that much. Yet that is precisely the love that God's people are meant to provide.

This is why in worship we are given the perfect love of God in Christ, a home of grace that cannot be removed: "I am convinced that neither death, nor life, nor angels, nor rulers, nor things present, nor things to come, nor powers, nor height, nor depth, nor anything else in all creation, will be able to separate us from the love of God in Christ Jesus our Lord" (Romans 8:38-39). But the purpose, this side of glory, for dwelling in such love and finding it so profoundly strong and all-sufficient is for the assurance we have in giving it away.

The consequence of this unshakable love of God is that it sets us free from the compulsion we have to protect and provide for ourselves, so instead we can turn our hearts and energies toward others. When we are held by the unbreakable lifeline of Jesus Christ, we can reach out to others who need it. It's how our faith is to be shown:

> What good is it, my brothers and sisters, if you say you have faith but do not have works? Can faith save you? If a brother or sister is naked and lacks daily food, and one of you says to them, "Go in peace; keep warm and eat your fill," and yet you do not supply their bodily needs, what is the good of that? So faith by itself, if it has no works, is dead. (James 2:14-17)

James says wake up! Live God's call to worship by doing justice, loving kindness and walking humbly with your God.

Where Are We?

The question that presses upon me most is this: are we who follow Jesus Christ believing and acting out what God considers the matters of first importance? Or are we, as I fear, asleep to the real passions of God and the real needs of the world? More specifically, do our lives and practices of worship lead us to live in the ways that matter to God?

These points are clear to me:

1. The kingdom of God is not a utopian vision, a dream with no hope of reality, but the assured and coming reign of Christ that will establish a new heaven and a new earth.

2. God is the one who ushers in the kingdom of righteousness and justice through Jesus Christ and by the Holy Spirit.

3. The church is God's primary witness to this coming kingdom but is not responsible for accomplishing it.

4. The church's worship of God should show up in love and justice for the sake of the poor, the needy, the oppressed and the forgotten.

What's more, we need to continue to grapple with whether our faith or our culture shapes our lives more. What are the distinctives that might lead us individually or as a community to live more kingdomlike lives? Here are some helpful questions for self-examination or small-group discussion:

• Are we ready to live life in God in our town, or do we still insist on living in our town and try to fit God in? Are we convinced that these two options are not the same thing? Are we convinced that God's serious plan for healing the nations in Jesus Christ involves us? That it means picking up our cross and laying down our claim to ourselves in real sacrifice, and that it will change our lives?

- Are we going to let our class, race, job or money set the terms and priorities of our life, or do we want to be seriously kingdom-minded and kingdom-hearted?

- Are we willing to let the gospel do the deep redefining work of establishing us in our new humanity, or will we only let it do a little sprucing up?

- Are we willing to let Sabbath-keeping redefine the weekly rhythms of our lives, calling us to lay down our activities, cease our multi-tasking, stop our consumption, recalibrate our priorities and redefine—for the sake of truly seeking God, for listening differently and intently for the Spirit, for remembering the passions of God for love, justice and mercy? Are we ready to seek God in our personal and corporate worship so we live to God's great honor?

- Are we willing to do the hard work of thinking beyond the categories of conservative and liberal in order to allow the kingdom to reorder the categories of issues that matter and that escape easy categorization? Are we willing to do the hard work of acting out the consequences of seeking justice, even when the cost is that our sense of self and life is fundamentally altered?

At a recent leadership retreat with the elders of our congregation, we began one evening with a time of silence during which each person was to reflect on one of their major soapbox issues. If they could make an appeal to others on a subject that deeply mattered to them, what would it be? Then I invited anyone who wanted to, to share what their issue was and why it mattered to them so much.

I had no idea that all thirty of the elders would want to speak, nor that it would take well over two hours, nor that it would become one of the most profound experiences we ever shared as a leadership team. A range of concerns was expressed, with the majority of them having to do with the intersection of various social needs and the gospel, some local, many national, still more international. It was moving to see people give such tender and heartfelt voice to their heart for the world around them.

We closed the exercise, which had become a holy moment, with extended prayer for the issues raised. Then we all agreed that before we met again two weeks later, we would each do something to take some concrete action about our soapbox issue and be ready to share what we had done. I was amazed at everyone's energy and eagerness to take this next step and by the importance of the things that had been accomplished just two weeks later. God gives his people his passions. And the energy of our lives, under the guidance of the Holy Spirit, can take our ordinary lives and make a significant difference when they are available.

When I think about our congregation, I am first of all aware of the ordinary and life-changing examples many of our members are to me. They simply get on with the quiet acts of justice that are the signs of grace and courage, compassion and commitment, that occur all the time in homes, classrooms, neighborhoods, offices, labs and towns, sometimes even beyond. I appreciate that they are a self-effacing community, not drawn to or swept up in self-promotion. Often I only happen to stumble upon the discovery of how long and faithfully they have been seeking justice in the ways God has called them.

Friendship is the most common doorway through which these church members have come to engage various justice issues. I think of the invisible bridge to property and rights some of them built for Japanese friends during the injustice of their internment. They walked together and stood utterly faithful in protecting and defending the rights and property of their friends when national hysteria denied them their liberty and abused their dignity. Some have been tutors and mentors, big brothers and big sisters, child advocates, classroom volunteers, youth leaders, drop-in clinic doctors and nurses, cooks and servers for the homeless, Bible study facilitators. They have done this over the long haul, through all kinds of seasons and challenges; they have persisted in joy and in pain, and they have done so because of Jesus Christ's call on their life. They have demonstrated our Lord's commitment to justice in the lives of those they have served.

I think of the acts of justice carried out every day in our public school classrooms. Well over one hundred members of our congregation are teachers who put themselves on the line day in and day out for individual children. In the midst of the children's powerlessness, some of our teachers are often among the only advocates in such children's lives. In response to the injustice of their home lives—often surrounded by violence, crime, drugs, poverty and abuse—people in our congregation have chosen to listen, promote, advocate, love, defend and support them. They have suffered with these who are among the forgotten.

Then there are those who have gone to city council meetings or state legislature hearings or demonstrations; those who have written letters to various representatives; those who have visited prisoners; those who have provided for the shelter and education of untouchable children in India; those who have have built houses in places around the world for people without shelter; those who have traveled to serve in prisons and refugee camps in Africa and Asia; those who have formed friendships with adults, youth and children on the streets of Berkeley; those who have advocated for children to get out of indentured slavery or to escape the clutches of the sex trade; those who have written checks to help provide support and resources.

We are not unique in these actions, of course. No doubt we are just learners who have a long way to go to enact God's heart for worship or for justice. Many individuals and congregations are further along in these matters than we are. Still, measured by such standards of activity, it does seem we are at least awakening. Yet we in the American church have some hard questions to ask ourselves. Can it not be said nonetheless that we are still a middle-class people in our life and our acts of justice more than we are a kingdom people? Can it yet be said that the kingdom shapes us more than our social class, either institutionally or individually? Do the signs of justice we enact show the distinct mark of Jesus, or are they just the signs of a relatively elevated social conscience with a little gospel inspiration thrown in? Will we act and not just think about acting? The journey continues.

Epilogue

WHAT'S AT STAKE IN WORSHIP? EVERYTHING. The urgent, indeed troubling, message of Scripture is that everything that matters is at stake in worship.

This book is an urgent appeal to be people who heed God's call to a lifestyle of worship that does justice. Will we worship God with the whole of our lives so that the work of justice becomes our bedrock testimony to the presence and power of Jesus Christ, whom we serve and worship?

My argument here is that this neglected and forgotten calling is central to God's character, to the revelation of God in Jesus Christ and to the church's witness to God's kingdom. The white, middle-class American church especially seems to be asleep to these things, which Scripture says matter most to God. We rancorously engage in worship wars that have more to do with form and our quest for cultural relevance than with our desire to be conformed to the life, character and actions of Jesus Christ. Sadly, that may be the church at its most awake! Even more often, we are just preoccupied with matters of our own institutional existence. We fall prey to a false discipleship that baptizes culture rather than living out a true discipleship that demonstrates our baptism by seeking to do justice, love mercy and walk humbly with our God.

The relationship between faith and culture is inescapable and complicated. Every believer, whatever the context, has always faced and always will face the dilemma of how to live in the world but not of the world.

Given the inescapability of culture, Christians tend to live life in terms of the culture with a splash of the gospel added to the mix. The call to mature discipleship, however, is meant to be one in which we seek to "take every thought captive to obey Christ" (2 Corinthians 10:5) and to bear the fruit of the Spirit in tangible action by visiting the prisoner, remembering the widow, feeding the hungry, serving the oppressed.

In other words, we are to live as exiles seeking above all else to be faithful imitators of the peculiar life and heart of the One we follow. Right in the midst of our Babylon, we are meant to show that we seek to live in and live out the life of the God we worship. It's about devoting ourselves to the dangerous act of worship, which means living God's call to justice.

Study Guide

THIS DISCUSSION GUIDE CAN BE USED TO FACILITATE a small group or Sunday school class based on *The Dangerous Act of Worship*. If members of the group are all reading the book, in addition to the following discussion questions, leaders may also ask questions like, "What parts of this chapter struck you the most? Did you underline or highlight anything that was particularly meaningful to you? Why?" These questions may also be used by individuals to help work through and apply the concepts of the book.

Chapter One: What's at Stake in Worship?

1. What comes to mind when you hear the word *worship?* What kinds of images or associations does it evoke? Why?

2. How is *worship* defined in this chapter?

3. How is this definition of *worship* similar to or different from the one you usually have in mind when you use the word?

4. If God sees worship in this encompassing way, what signs do you see that many in the church are asleep rather than awake to God's purposes for worship?

5. What do the prophets and Jesus say is at stake if God's people are asleep rather than awake to God's purposes?

6. What would the church look like if it were really awake to God's purposes through worship?

7. In what ways do you struggle to wake up and live out this kind of worship?

8. What would need to change for you to live and worship more wakefully?

Chapter Two: The Real Battle over Worship

1. Preferences about worship can often be both unifying and dividing to the body of Christ. What examples have you seen of this?

2. What kinds of worship issues upset people the most? Why do you think that is so?

3. According to this chapter, what is the central human battle over worship really about? How does it contrast with many of our preoccupations about worship?

4. If worship is the enactment of what are to be our two great loves, for God and our neighbor, why and in what ways are they inseparable? Why do we nevertheless forget or separate them?

5. Consider Isaiah 1:12-17. How does our worship measure up to this standard?

6. How is worship meant to reorder our lives?

7. How would you need to approach worship in your life in order for it to have this effect? What primary things would need to be altered in your life?

8. How motivated are you to face and respond to the real battle over worship? What are you willing to do about it? Who else might join you in doing so?

Chapter Three: False Dangers

1. What experience have you had of fearing something that turned out to be no real danger? How did you come to realize that?

2. What is meant in this chapter by "false dangers" related to worship?

What makes them false?

3. What are the consequences for Christian discipleship and mission in the world if we are absorbed by fearing the wrong dangers? What are examples you see?

4. Consider each of the false dangers in turn and summarize what they are naming. Choose one or two of them, and discuss:

    a. How do you see evidences of each one?

    b. Which one(s) most characterize your life?

    c. Which most affects the life of your congregation? Why?

    d. What would need to happen for your worship of God to unmask these false dangers—for you personally? For your small group? For your congregation?

5. Reordering our worship lives and unmasking these false dangers is central for our faith to mature. It is truly a spiritual change, not merely a mechanical or liturgical one. How might you commit to and pray for this transformation for yourself and for your congregation?

6. Who else could join you in this intercession? Conclude your time together by praying about these issues.

Chapter Four: Real Dangers

1. What is some genuine danger that you feel you have good reasons to fear? Why?

2. What role does fear have in your knowledge or experience of God? What is healthy about that, and what is unhealthy?

3. What is meant in this chapter by "real dangers" related to worship? What makes them real?

4. In what sense is worship of the living God dangerous? In what ways does the Bible testify to that reality? (How does this relate to God's grace?)

5. What experiences of God have you had that you understood to be dangerous (i.e., confronting or changing you, your relationships or your priorities in ways that require you becoming a new creature in Christ)?

6. Consider each of the real dangers in turn and summarize what they are naming. Choose one or two of them and discuss:

   a. How do you see (or fail to see) evidences of each one?

   b. Which one(s) most characterize your life?

   c. Which most affects the life of your congregation? Why?

   d. Which one(s) do you wish more fully characterized your encounter with God or your church's encounter? How might that happen?

7. In what ways do you try to domesticate God for your comfort?

8. How might the good blessing of an encounter with the living and dangerous God help you engage more passionately in a life of justice and righteousness?

9. What could help you grow in your vision of God? What steps are you willing to take?

Chapter Five: Waking Up to Where We Live

1. When have you experienced a big move? What feelings did you have going through the adjustment? Why did you feel that way?

2. What do you think the author means by saying that "the gospel re-contextualizes where we live" (p. 79)?

3. In what ways does being "in Christ" give us a new address in the world?

4. Try writing out your "address." What adjectives or descriptors (home address, race, education, work, power, etc.) tell others or yourself the most important things about "where" you live?

5. Now put those words in some order of influence. If you are a follower

of Jesus, how do these factors relate to your now being "in Christ"?

6. How does dwelling in the life of the triune God create a new neighborhood in our lives?

7. Do your worship practices (both individual and corporate) help wake you up to where God now wants us to live? Why or why not? How does it change your "neighborhood"?

8. How might you move into your life in God more deeply?

9. How might this help you come to know your neighbors better? How would it be an act of worship to do so? What steps could you take toward loving those neighbors as yourself?

Chapter Six: Doing Justice Starts with Rest

1. What do you do when you want deep rest? What most renews you?

2. If doing justice involves action, how and why does doing justice start with rest?

3. How does a biblical Sabbath relate to justice?

4. What does living in God's rest mean to you? How does it relate to your worship of God? How does it relate to your trying to do justice in the world?

5. Do you have Sabbath practices in your life? If so, what are they? Why do you observe them?

6. Are these practices releasing and renewing to your life of worship through the week? Why or why not?

7. As a follower of Jesus, do you live knowing and practicing the freedom to say yes and to say no? Which is easier or harder for you? Why?

8. How do you need encouragement to practice both words, *yes* and *no*? How can you encourage others to do so as well?

Chapter Seven: When Worship Talks to Power

1. When was the last time you saw yourself or someone else confronting some form of power by calling it into question? What are typical ways of doing so?

2. According to the argument of this chapter, how does worship define and confront power?

3. If "Jesus is Lord," how does that define a Christian's understanding of power in the world?

4. Try to summarize the heart of problems with power in the world. What windows does the Bible give into the nature of power abuse and injustice?

5. How could our practice of worship help us as followers of Jesus to see power realigned in our lives?

6. As you look through the list of classical elements of a service of worship, which ones stand out for you? Why?

7. Which ones do you most need to confront power issues in your life and circumstances?

8. Does your experience of corporate worship, whatever the liturgy, help you have a more biblically responsible grasp of issues of power in your life and the world?

9. How can you encourage and practice this more fully in your own life? in your community of faith?

Chapter Eight: Dwelling in Exodus or in Exile?

1. When was the last time you were "a long ways from home"? What did it feel like? What did you want to do about it? Why?

2. This chapter considers two seasons in Israel's life when they were not at home: their time in Egypt and the exodus, and their time in Babylon when God sent Israel into exile. In light of this chapter,

how would you define "life in Egypt"?

3. What is the New Testament's understanding of our continuing need for deliverance—for an exodus—from what and for what?

4. How does the exodus paradigm show itself in American culture?

5. How does exodus appear in your experience of the church? How does this paradigm help or hinder the American church's response to injustice?

6. How would you define "life in exile"?

7. What is the New Testament's understanding of our continuing need to acknowledge that we are "strangers and aliens"?

8. How does the exile paradigm show its presence or absence in society? in your experience of the church?

9. What does the theme of exile prod you to consider or to do differently about issues of justice?

10. How does your experience of worship help you live as a faithful exile following Jesus? How does it help you seek justice for others?

11. What would help your response to mature and express itself even more?

Chapter Nine: An Imagination for Justice

1. What kinds of things most engage your imagination? Why?

2. Before reading this chapter, how would you have described the relationship between worship, justice and imagination?

3. According to this chapter, what makes imagination so important in matters of worship and justice?

4. How does your experience of worship stimulate or fail to stimulate your imagination for God or things of God? Why?

5. How does this affect your life as a disciple who seeks and does justice?

6. How is your imagination triggered by personal or corporate worship to respond to the needs of the poor, the oppressed or the needy? Why?

7. How could this be more provoked? How actively do you allow yourself to step into the pain and need of others?

8. How can you keep your imagination growing for God and for God's heart for justice?

9. What will help you do that? How might your personal, small group or congregational worship practices help?

Chapter Ten: Living Awake

1. Living awake to God and the world may sound like God's call, but we are all tempted to stay asleep to such life-challenging encounters. How are you are tempted to "sleep" rather than fully wake up and engage in worship that does justice?

2. This chapter offers a series of choices: the choice to live our worship, the choice to see, the choice to engage and the choice to love. What do each of these mean? Which one(s) do you think you have embraced and tried to live? Which one(s) do you have yet to enact?

3. Which of these choices do others say that they actually see you living out? How?

4. If you were to describe a year from now how you are living awake to God and to God's concerns for worship that does justice, what would you want to be able to say or show?

5. What will be necessary for these things to occur?

6. Who will you ask to join you in making these changes?

7. How can others stand with you in prayer for these things, and how can you do the same for them?

8. Concluding exercise: Set the alarm clock or make an appointment in your daily planner for a year from now and plan to meet with some friends to see how you are living awake by then.

Everything is at stake. This really matters. Worship by how you live.

Notes

Chapter 1: What's at Stake in Worship?
[1]United Nations Secretary General, The Millennium Project <www.millennium project.org>.

[2]According to *The State of the World's Children 2006: Excluded and Invisible* (New York: Unicef, 2005), p. 50, 1.2 million children are trafficked in the international sex trade per year.

Chapter 2: The Real Battle over Worship
[1]The Law prescribes the Sabbath and the Jubilee years (Leviticus 25) as ways of putting limits on what would otherwise lead to (and has led to) generations of poverty and suffering.

Chapter 3: False Dangers
[1]See especially the book of Leviticus.

[2]"Christian 'Idol' Show Set for Trinity," *Billboard,* June 18, 2004.

Chapter 4: Real Dangers
[1]John Calvin, *Institutes of the Christian Religion* 1.13.1.

[2]Annie Dillard, *Teaching a Stone to Talk: Expeditions and Encounters* (New York: Harper Collins, 1982), p. 40.

Chapter 5: Waking Up to Where We Live
[1]Paul Willis, "Children Scapegoated as Witches in Fallout from Congo's Civil War," *The San Francisco Chronicle,* July 9, 2006.

[2]C. S. Lewis, *The Weight of Glory* (New York: Harper Collins, 1949), p. 9.

Chapter 6: Doing Justice Starts with Rest
[1]Mother Teresa of Calcutta, *A Gift for God: Prayers and Meditations* (New York: Harper and Row, 1975), p. 40.

[2]The Malaria Control Programme, World Health Organization, *Third World Network Features, Health Canada,* The Centers for Disease Control and Prevention, and Desowitz Roberts, *The Malaria Capers: More Tales of Parasites and People, Research and Reality* (New York: W. W. Norton, 1991).

[3]According to *The State of the World's Children 2006: Excluded and Invisible* (New York: Unicef, 2005), p. 50; 1.2 million children are trafficked in the international sex trade each year.

Chapter 7: When Worship Talks to Power

[1]Richard Re, "A Persisting Evil: The Global Problem of Slavery," *Harvard International Review,* winter 2002.

[2]Joint Monitoring Programme for Water Supply and Sanitation (WHO and UNICEF), Millennium Development Goals Assessment Report, 2006.

[3]"Life Expectancy," Global Burden of Disease and Risk Factors (WHO), 2002.

[4]"With Pension System a Mess, China Calls Cato," *The Washington Post,* August 21, 2001.

Chapter 8: Dwelling in Exodus or in Exile?

[1]This term refers to what has often been called the Third World. The term "majority world" reflects that we are referring to the majority of the world's population, which lives in great poverty and need. The marginal are the majority.

Chapter 9: An Imagination for Justice

[1]Consult the website of International Justice Mission (ijm.org) to see the many outstanding resources IJM provides for personal and small group Bible study and reflection on a Christian view and practice of justice.

[2]Again, the creative resources of IJM (ijm.org) can be very helpful in stimulating our imagination for justice.

[3]*The Heidelberg Catechism,* response to question no. 1.

Chapter 10: Living Awake

[1]Mother Teresa of Calcutta, *A Gift for God: Prayers and Meditations* (New York: Harper & Row, 1975), p. 40.

[2]Blaise Pascal, *Pensées,* Pensee #919, in *Christianity for Modern Pagans: Pascal's Pensées,* ed. Peter Kreeft (San Francisco: Ignatius Press, 1992), p. 330.